I DRAW FASHION

INVERTED TRIANGLE FACE SHAPE

MAKEUP FACE CHARTS FOR MAKEUP ARTISTS

MODEL: WHITE

CONTENTS

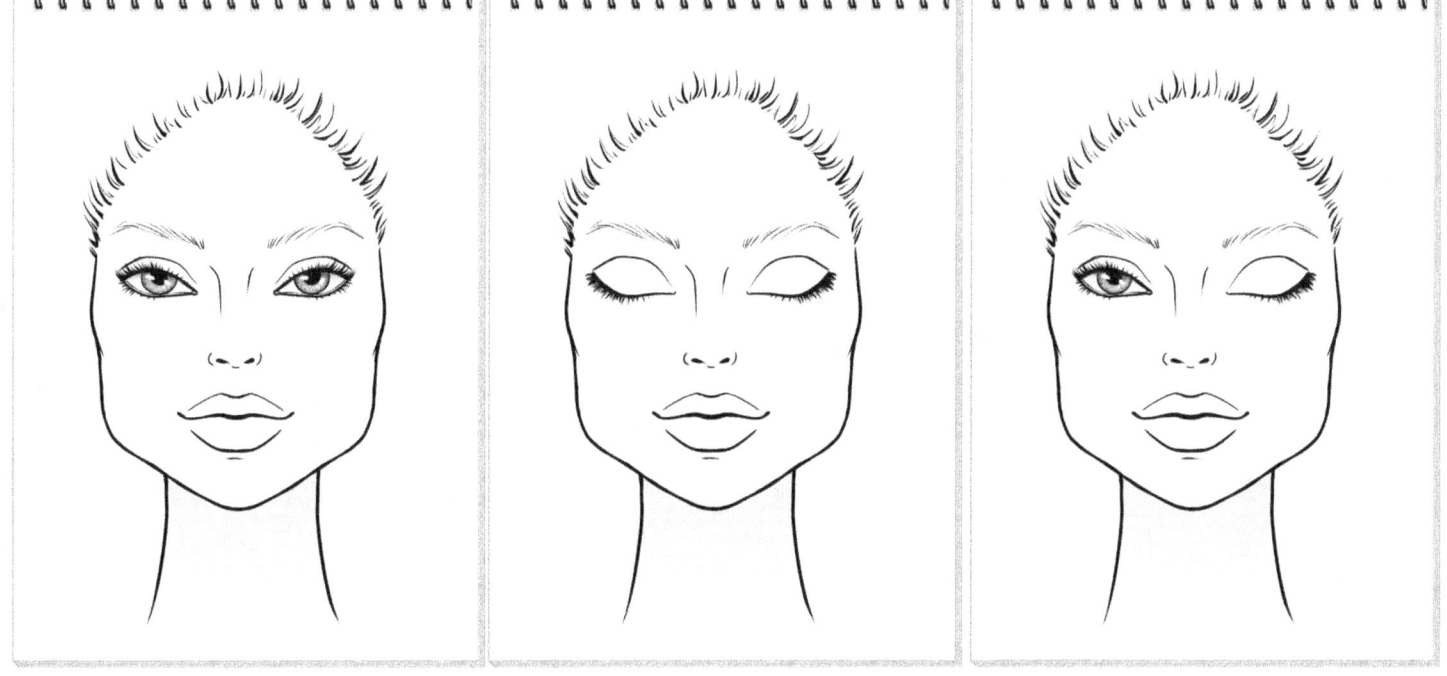

OPENED EYES
FACE CHARTS

PREPARATION

Cleanser

Moisturizer

Primer

FACE

Concealer

Foundation

Powder

Highlighter

Contour

Bronzer

Blush

EYES

Eyeshadow lid

Eyeshadow crease

Eyeliner

Mascara

Lashes

Brows

LIPS

Lip color

Lip liner

Lip gloss

OTHER

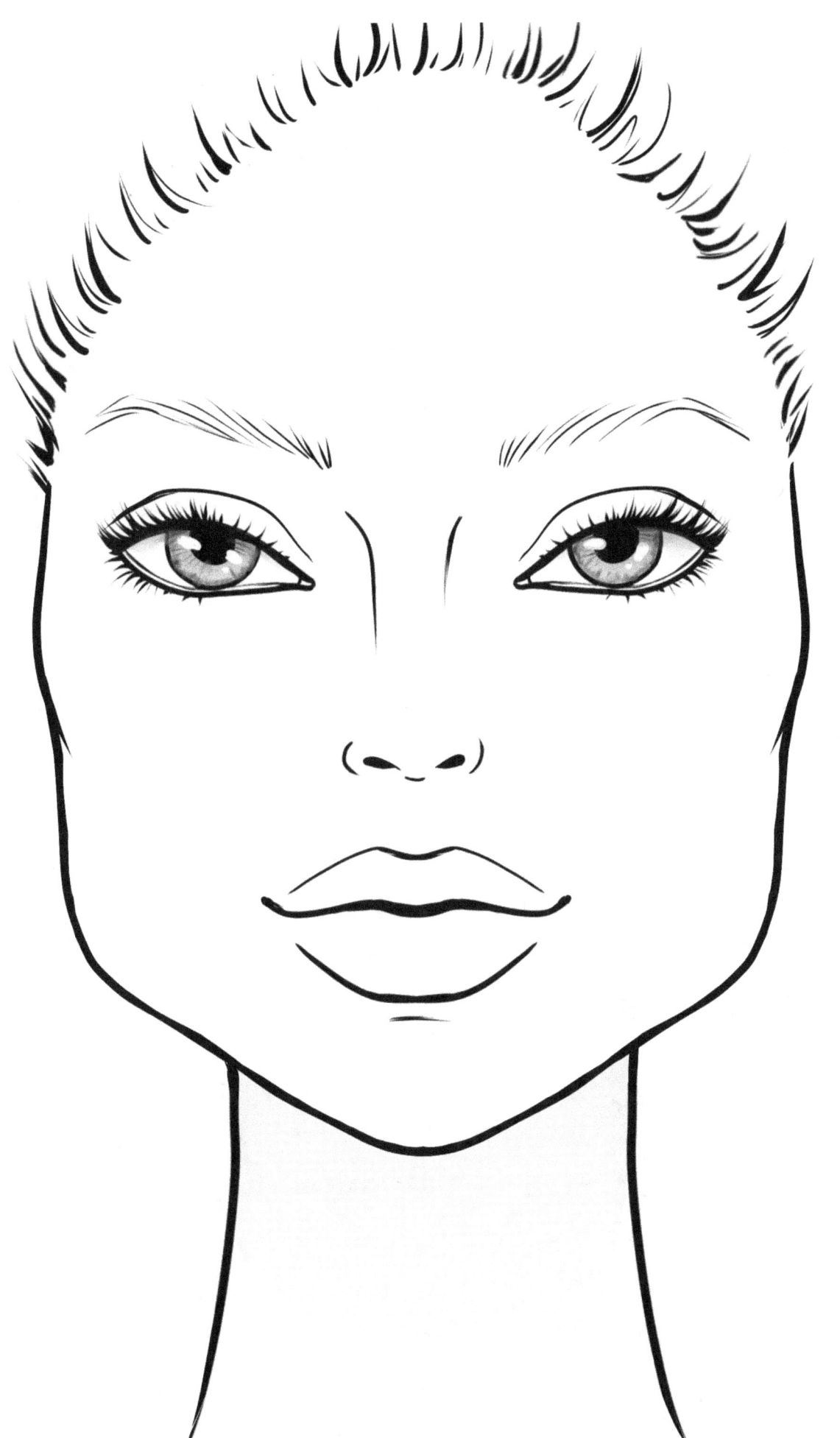

PREPARATION

Cleanser

Moisturizer

Primer

FACE

Concealer

Foundation

Powder

Highlighter

Contour

Bronzer

Blush

EYES

Eyeshadow lid

Eyeshadow crease

Eyeliner

Mascara

Lashes

Brows

LIPS

Lip color

Lip liner

Lip gloss

OTHER

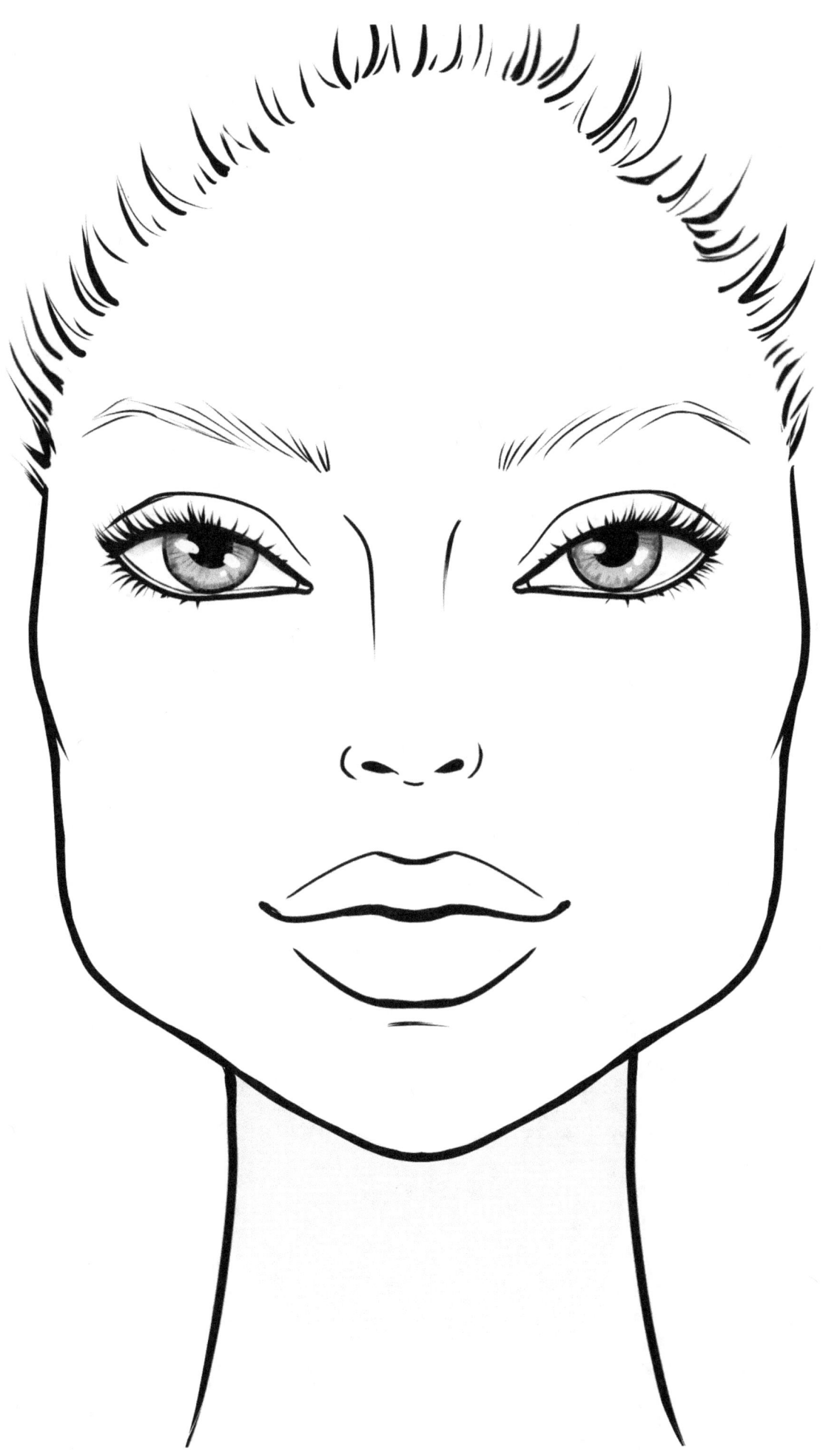

PREPARATION

Cleanser

Moisturizer

Primer

FACE

Concealer

Foundation

Powder

Highlighter

Contour

Bronzer

Blush

EYES

Eyeshadow lid

Eyeshadow crease

Eyeliner

Mascara

Lashes

Brows

LIPS

Lip color

Lip liner

Lip gloss

OTHER

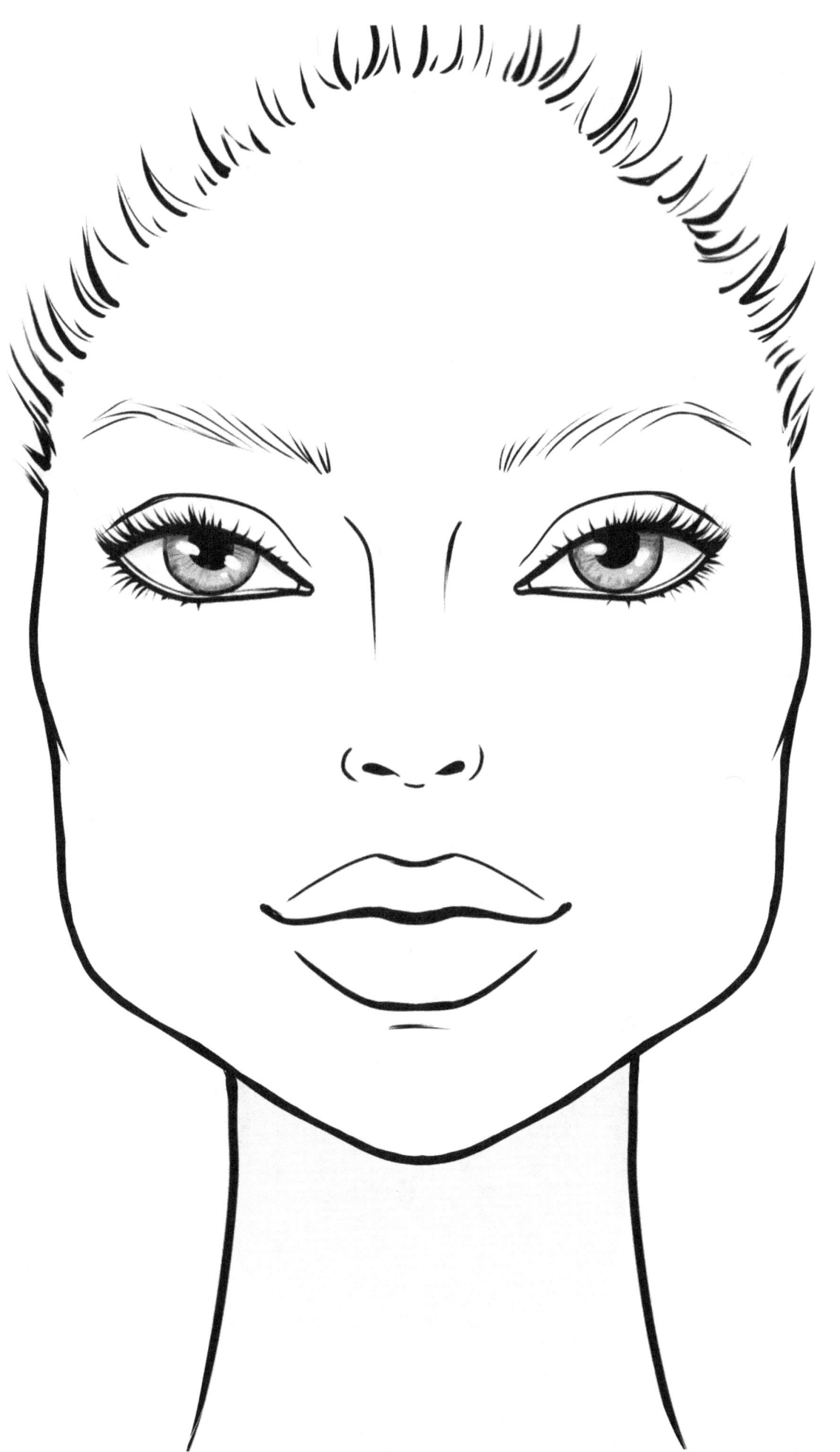

PREPARATION

Cleanser

Moisturizer

Primer

FACE

Concealer

Foundation

Powder

Highlighter

Contour

Bronzer

Blush

EYES

Eyeshadow lid

Eyeshadow crease

Eyeliner

Mascara

Lashes

Brows

LIPS

Lip color

Lip liner

Lip gloss

OTHER

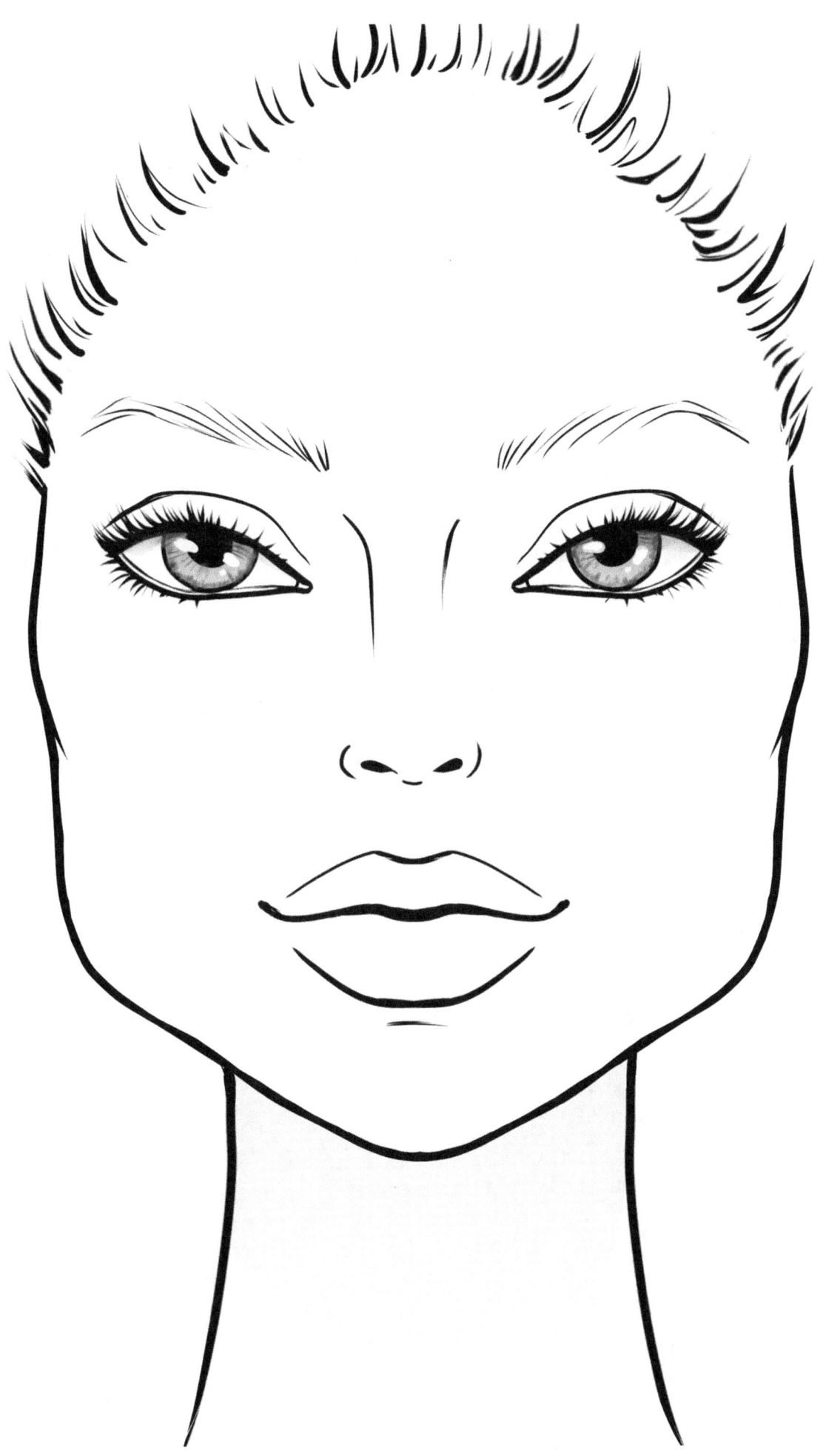

PREPARATION

Cleanser

Moisturizer

Primer

FACE

Concealer

Foundation

Powder

Highlighter

Contour

Bronzer

Blush

EYES

Eyeshadow lid

Eyeshadow crease

Eyeliner

Mascara

Lashes

Brows

LIPS

Lip color

Lip liner

Lip gloss

OTHER

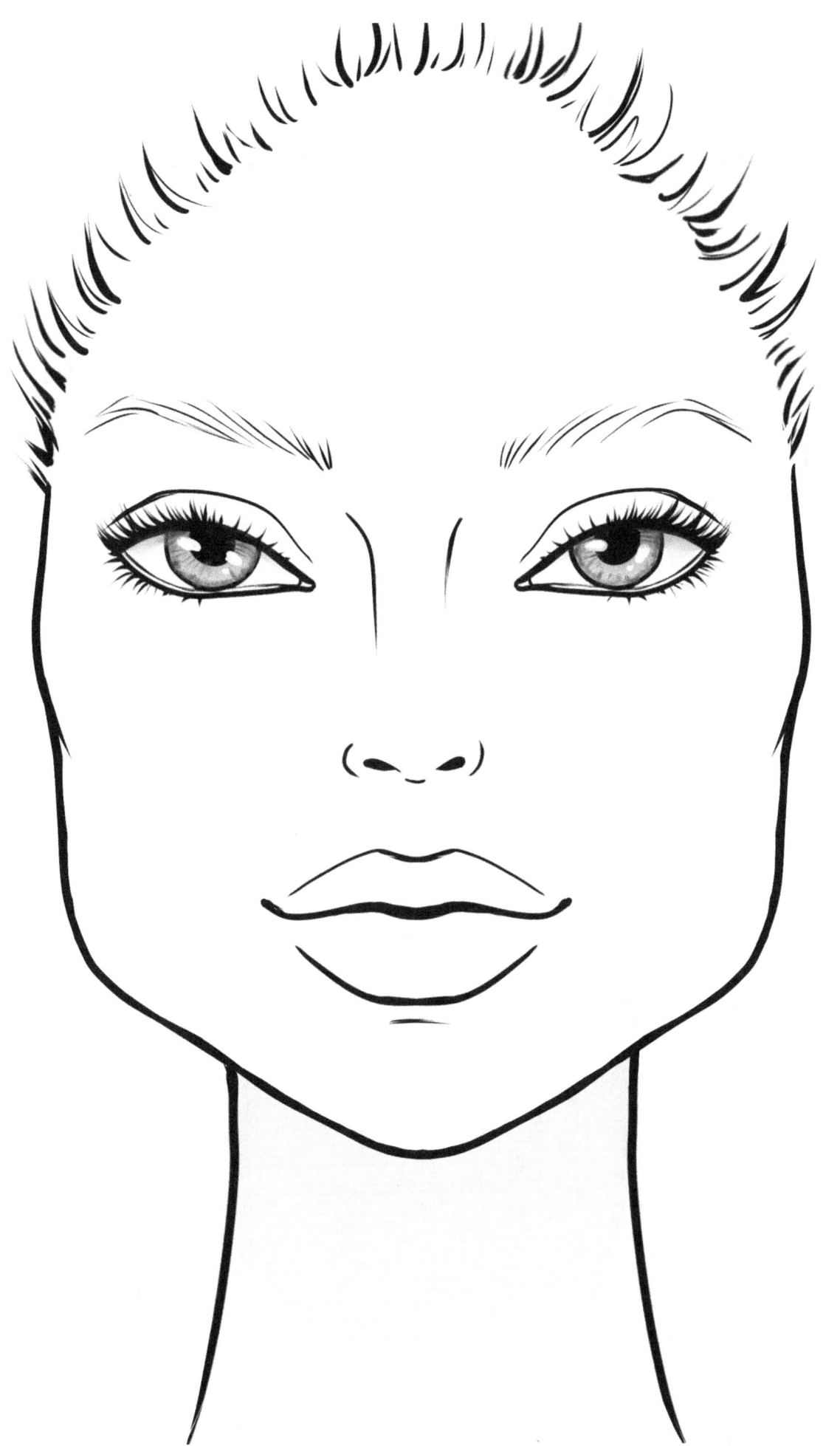

PREPARATION

Cleanser

Moisturizer

Primer

FACE

Concealer

Foundation

Powder

Highlighter

Contour

Bronzer

Blush

EYES

Eyeshadow lid

Eyeshadow crease

Eyeliner

Mascara

Lashes

Brows

LIPS

Lip color

Lip liner

Lip gloss

OTHER

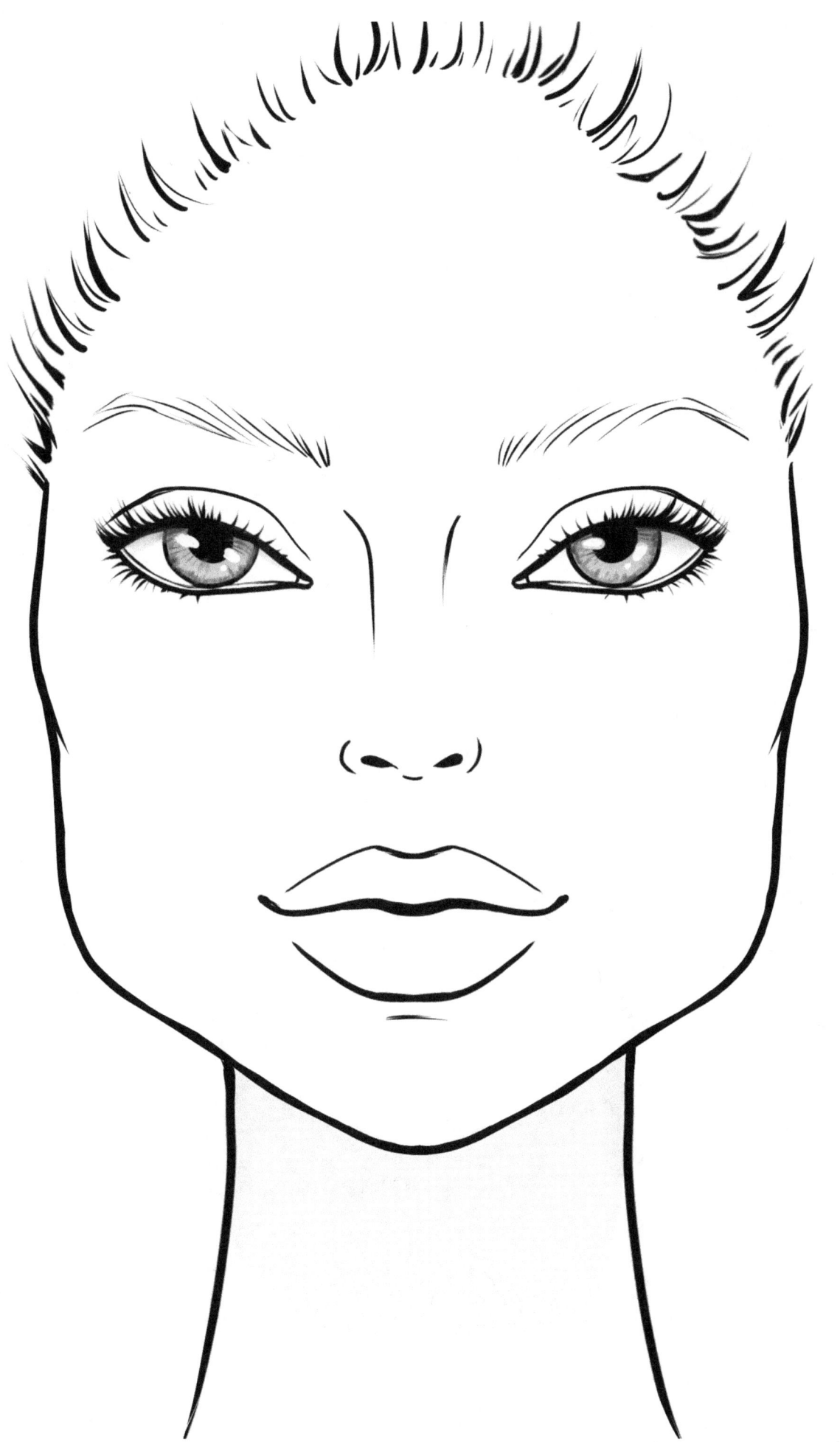

PREPARATION

Cleanser

Moisturizer

Primer

FACE

Concealer

Foundation

Powder

Highlighter

Contour

Bronzer

Blush

EYES

Eyeshadow lid

Eyeshadow crease

Eyeliner

Mascara

Lashes

Brows

LIPS

Lip color

Lip liner

Lip gloss

OTHER

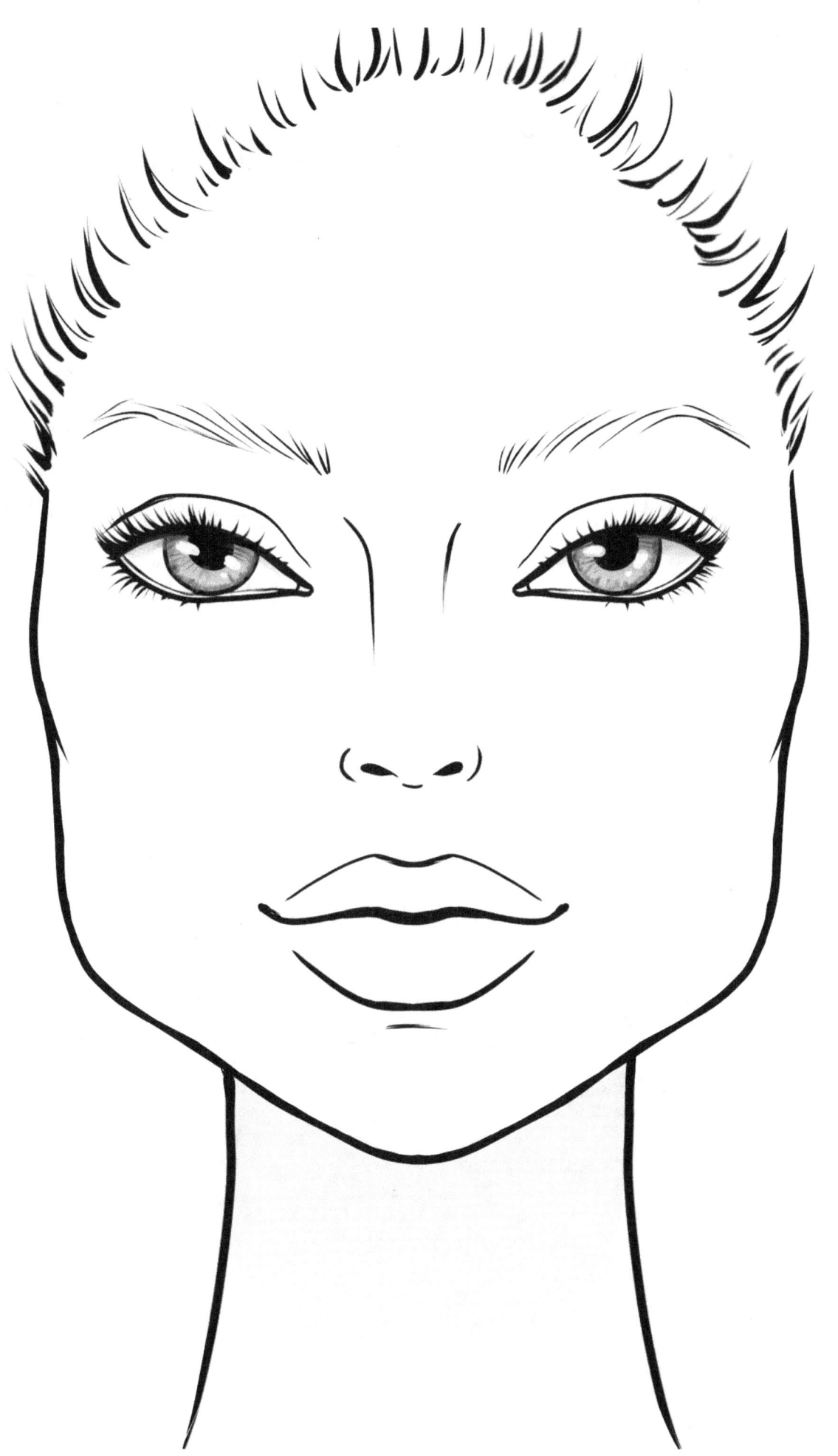

PREPARATION

Cleanser

Moisturizer

Primer

FACE

Concealer

Foundation

Powder

Highlighter

Contour

Bronzer

Blush

EYES

Eyeshadow lid

Eyeshadow crease

Eyeliner

Mascara

Lashes

Brows

LIPS

Lip color

Lip liner

Lip gloss

OTHER

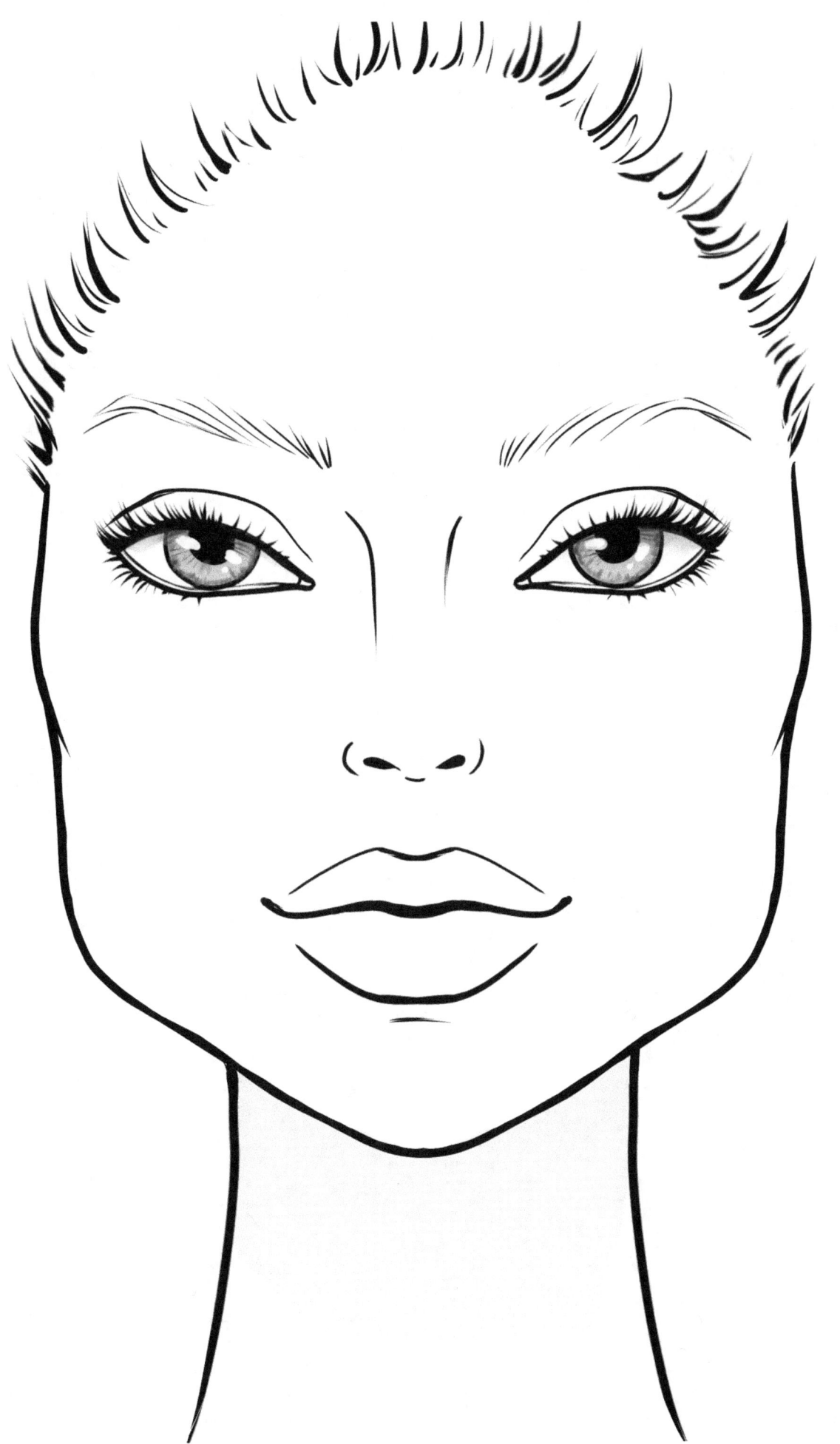

PREPARATION

Cleanser

Moisturizer

Primer

FACE

Concealer

Foundation

Powder

Highlighter

Contour

Bronzer

Blush

EYES

Eyeshadow lid

Eyeshadow crease

Eyeliner

Mascara

Lashes

Brows

LIPS

Lip color

Lip liner

Lip gloss

OTHER

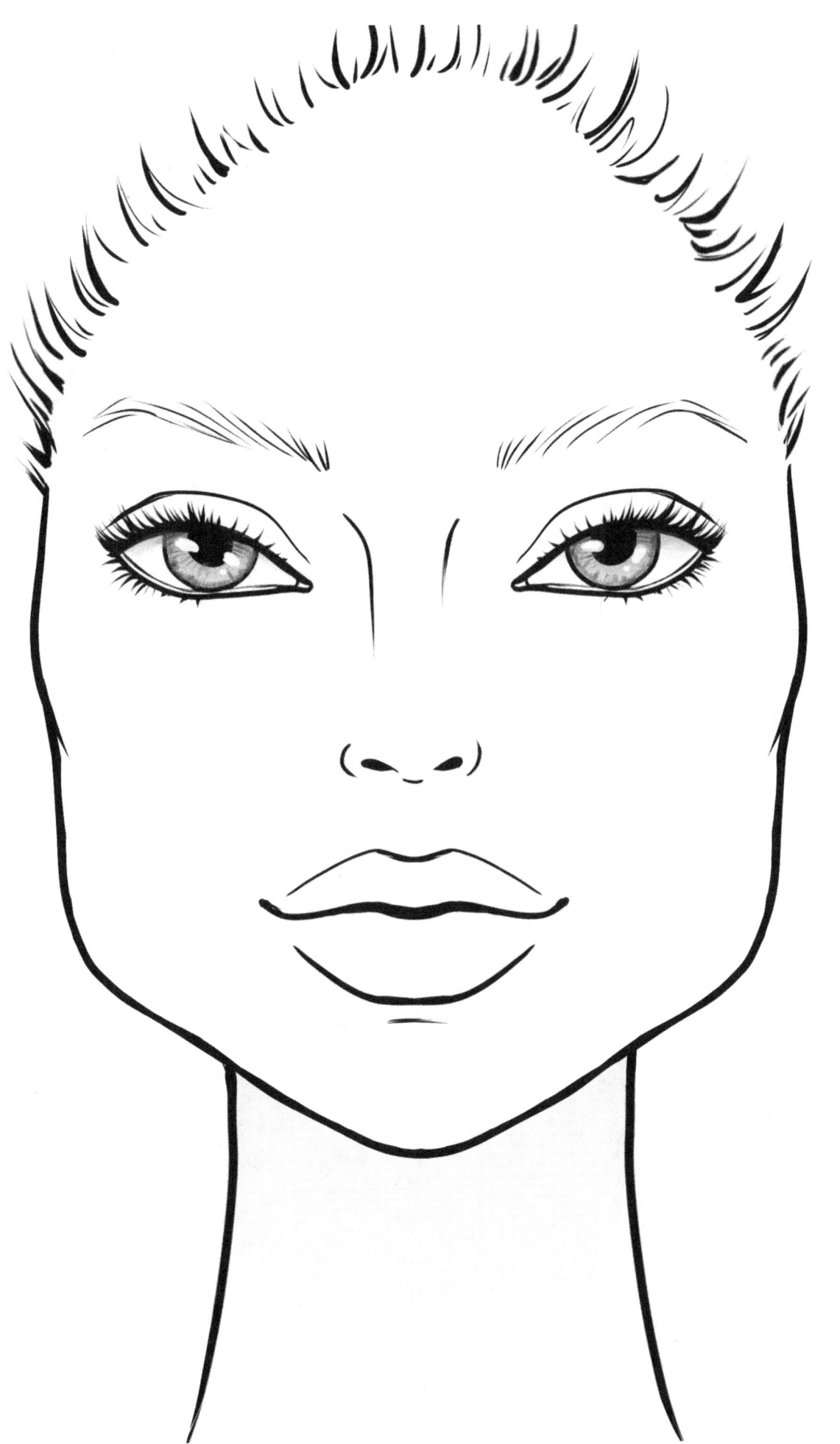

PREPARATION

Cleanser

Moisturizer

Primer

FACE

Concealer

Foundation

Powder

Highlighter

Contour

Bronzer

Blush

EYES

Eyeshadow lid

Eyeshadow crease

Eyeliner

Mascara

Lashes

Brows

LIPS

Lip color

Lip liner

Lip gloss

OTHER

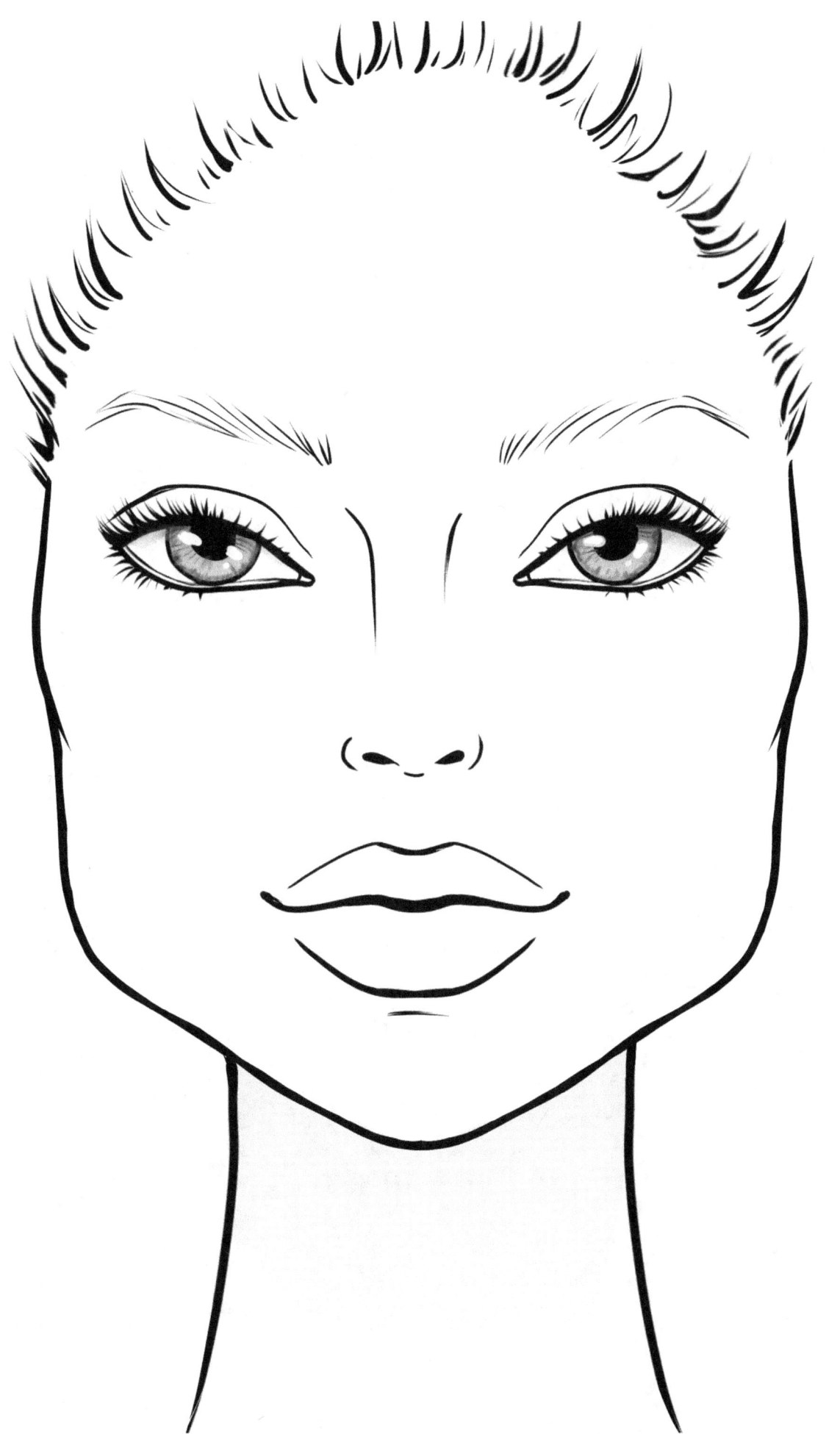

PREPARATION

Cleanser

Moisturizer

Primer

FACE

Concealer

Foundation

Powder

Highlighter

Contour

Bronzer

Blush

EYES

Eyeshadow lid

Eyeshadow crease

Eyeliner

Mascara

Lashes

Brows

LIPS

Lip color

Lip liner

Lip gloss

OTHER

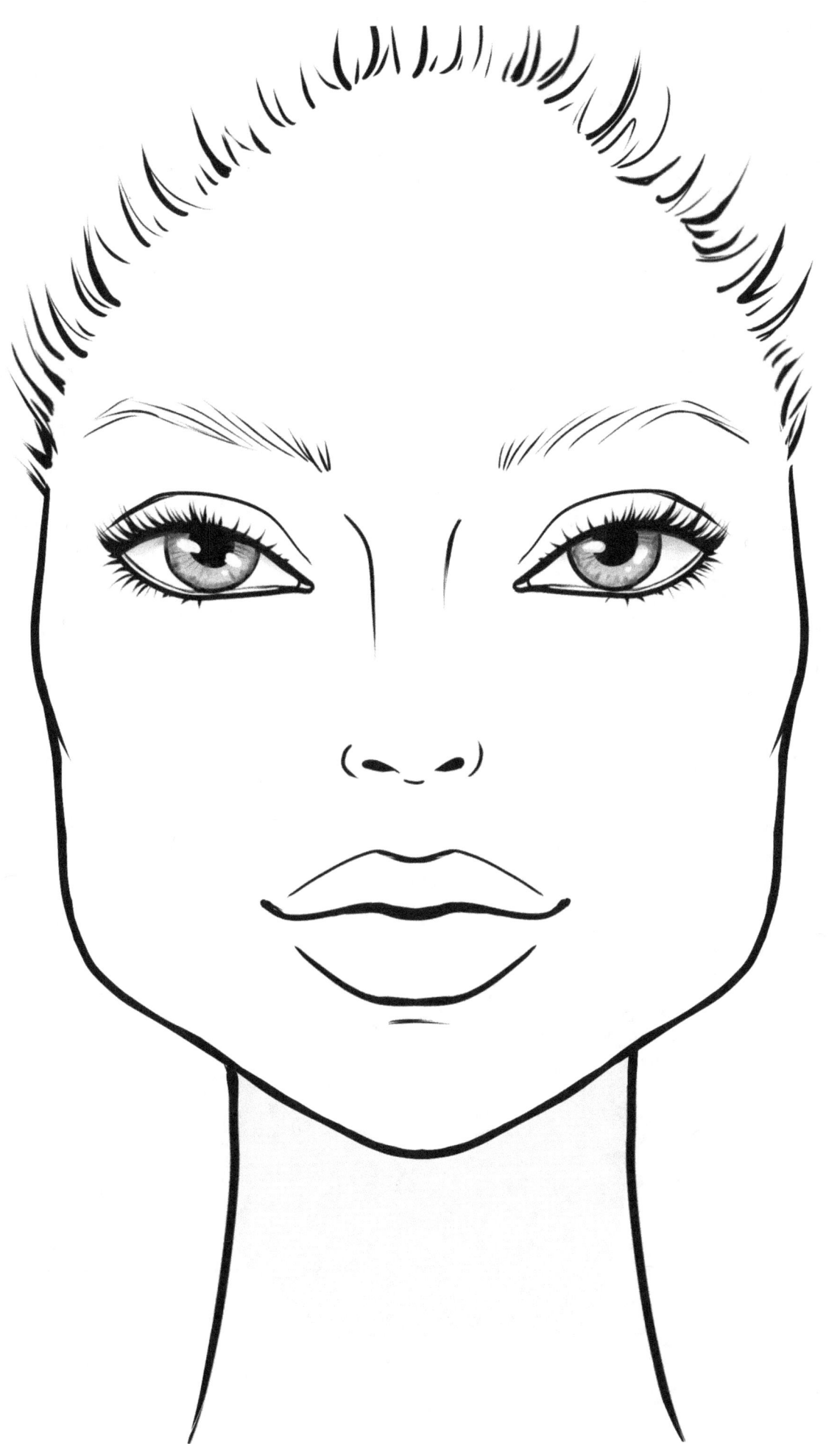

PREPARATION

Cleanser

Moisturizer

Primer

FACE

Concealer

Foundation

Powder

Highlighter

Contour

Bronzer

Blush

EYES

Eyeshadow lid

Eyeshadow crease

Eyeliner

Mascara

Lashes

Brows

LIPS

Lip color

Lip liner

Lip gloss

OTHER

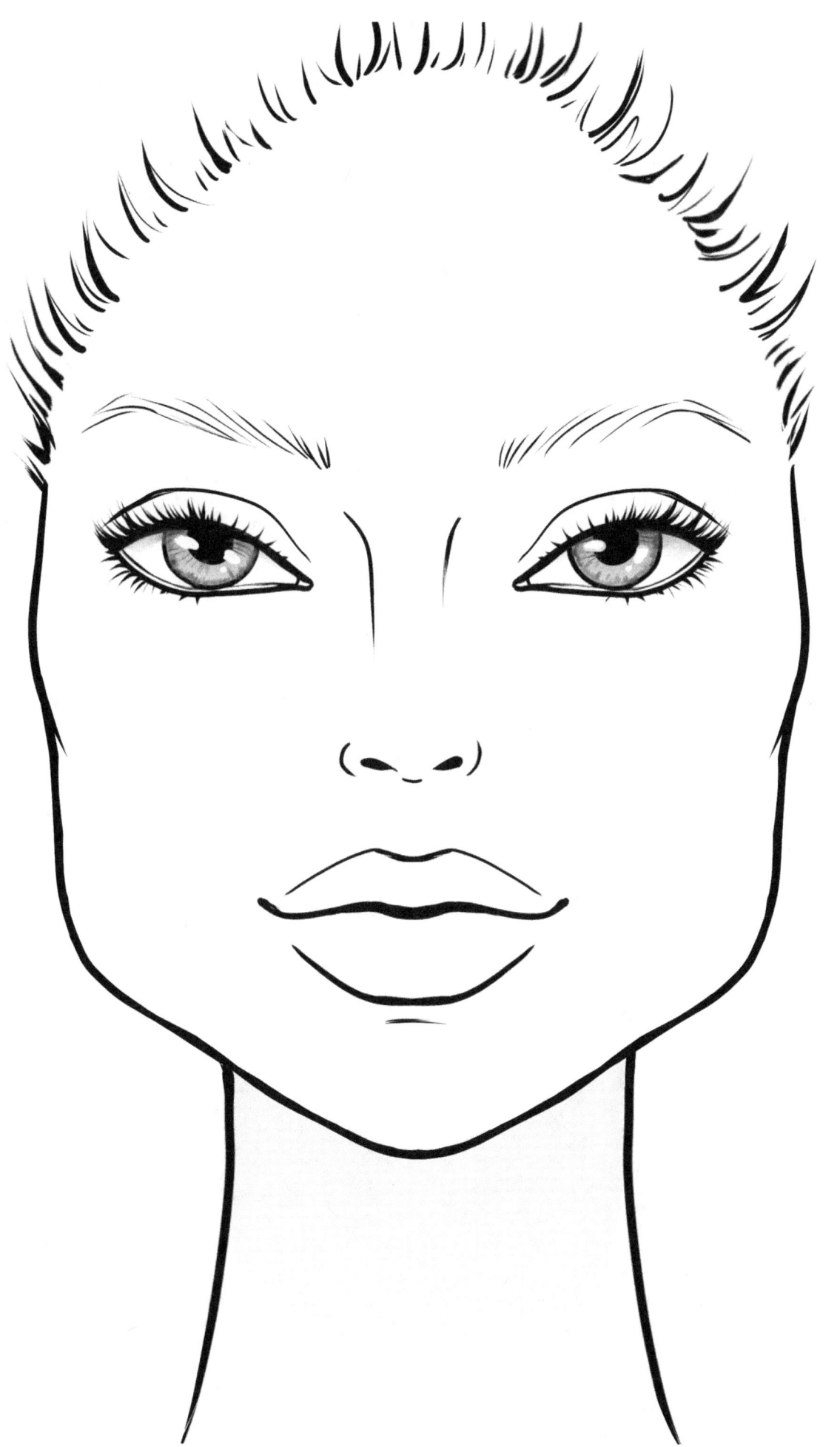

PREPARATION

Cleanser

Moisturizer

Primer

FACE

Concealer

Foundation

Powder

Highlighter

Contour

Bronzer

Blush

EYES

Eyeshadow lid

Eyeshadow crease

Eyeliner

Mascara

Lashes

Brows

LIPS

Lip color

Lip liner

Lip gloss

OTHER

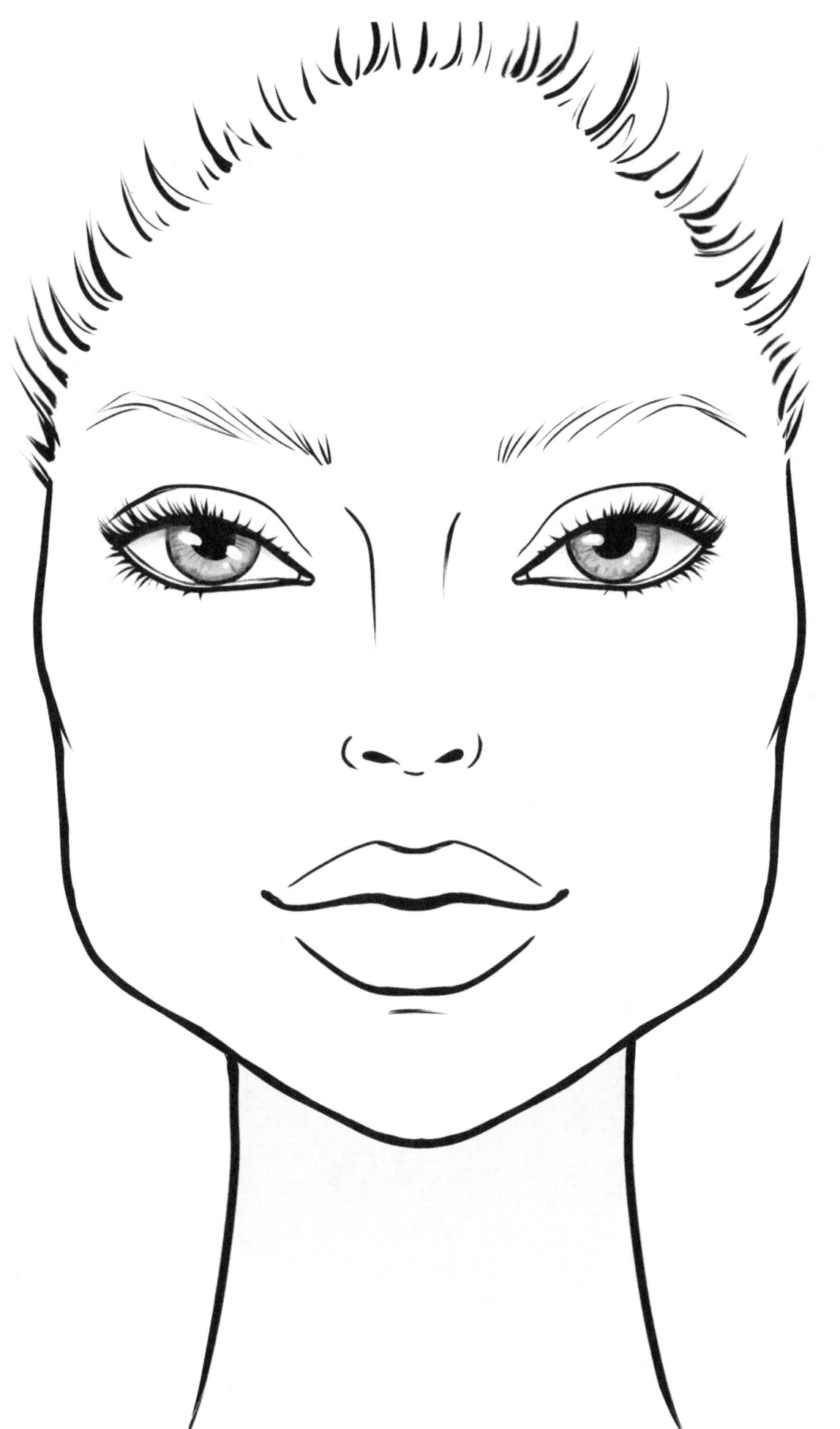

PREPARATION

Cleanser

Moisturizer

Primer

FACE

Concealer

Foundation

Powder

Highlighter

Contour

Bronzer

Blush

EYES

Eyeshadow lid

Eyeshadow crease

Eyeliner

Mascara

Lashes

Brows

LIPS

Lip color

Lip liner

Lip gloss

OTHER

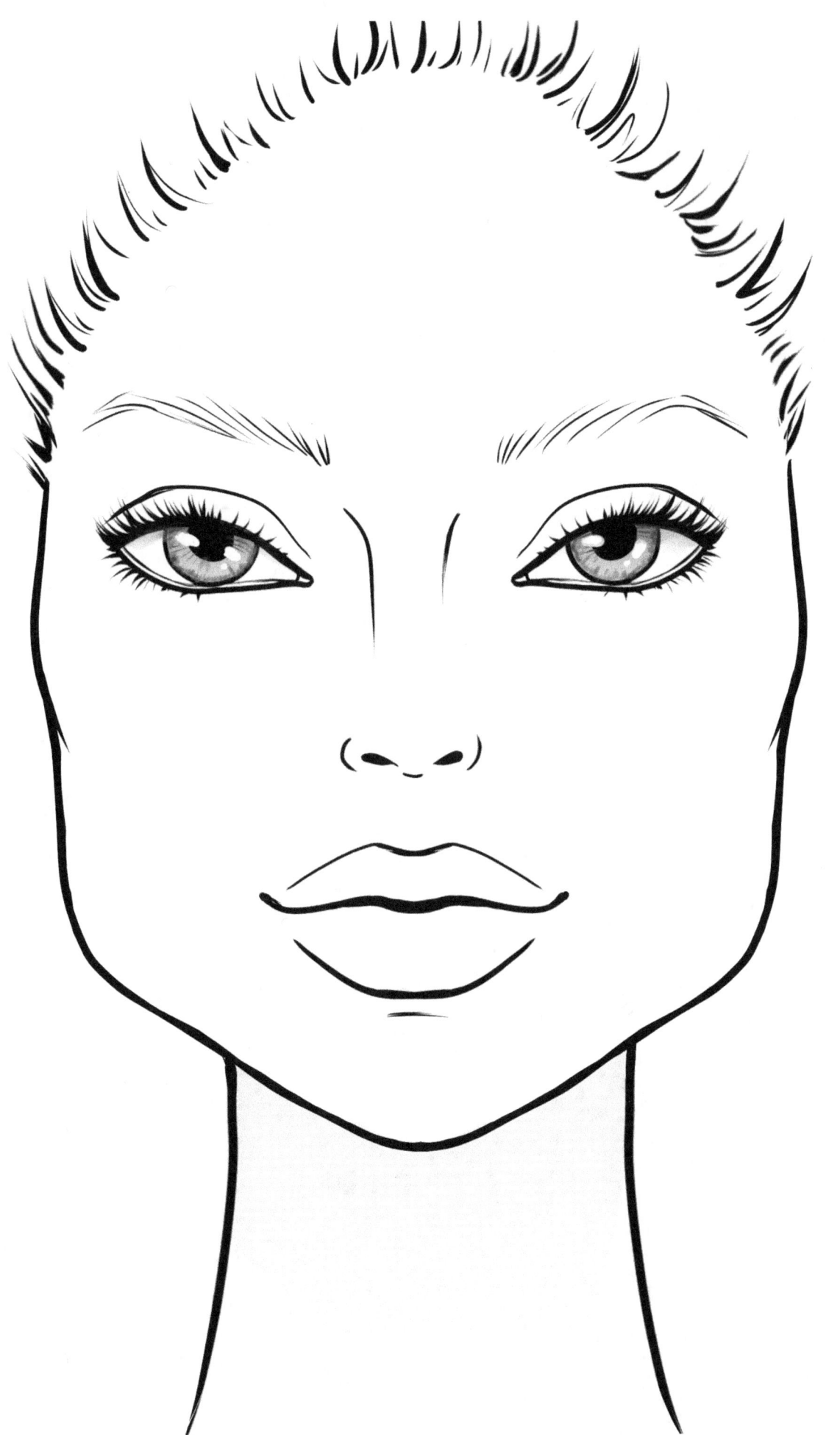

PREPARATION

Cleanser

Moisturizer

Primer

FACE

Concealer

Foundation

Powder

Highlighter

Contour

Bronzer

Blush

EYES

Eyeshadow lid

Eyeshadow crease

Eyeliner

Mascara

Lashes

Brows

LIPS

Lip color

Lip liner

Lip gloss

OTHER

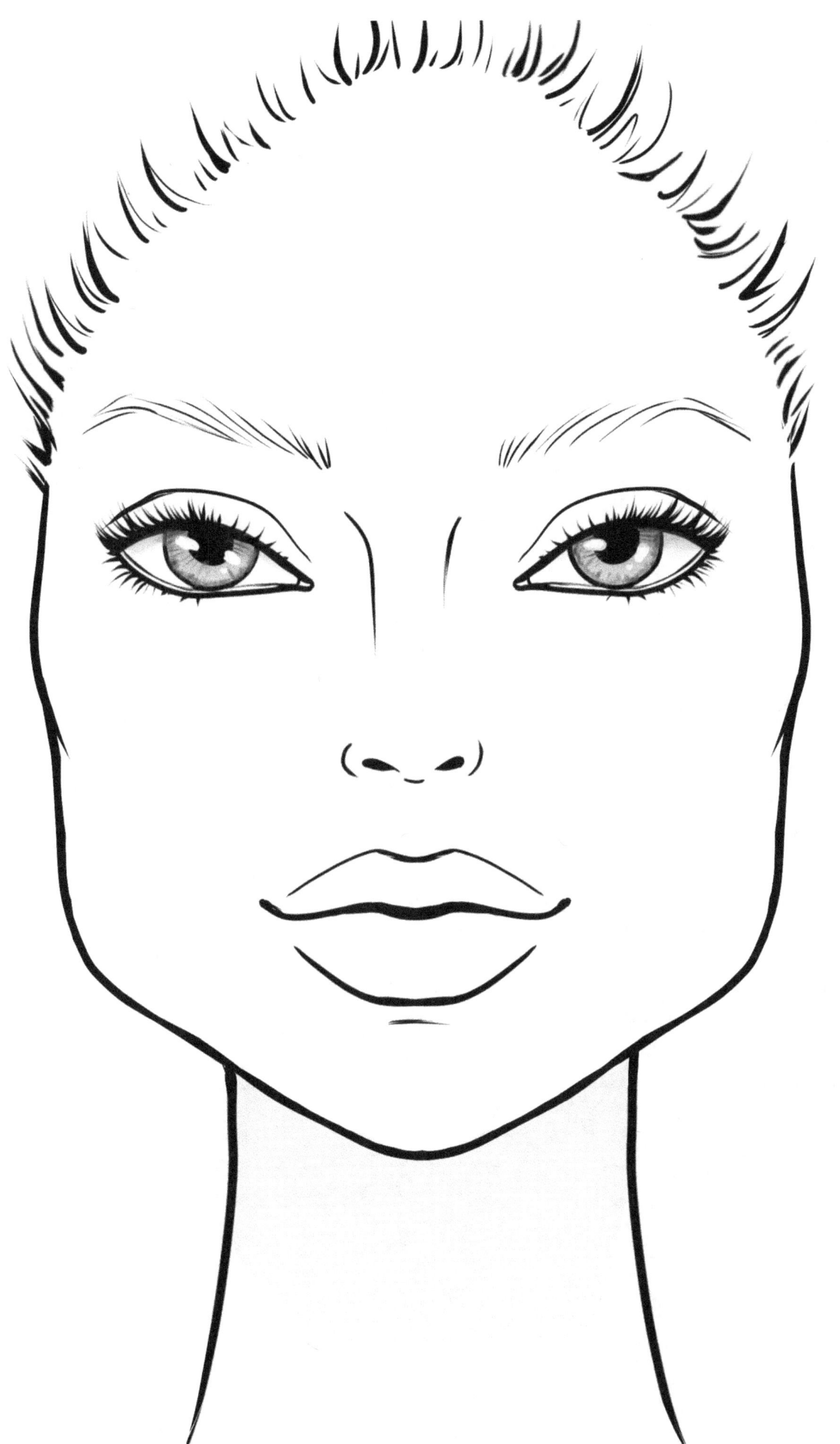

PREPARATION

Cleanser

Moisturizer

Primer

FACE

Concealer

Foundation

Powder

Highlighter

Contour

Bronzer

Blush

EYES

Eyeshadow lid

Eyeshadow crease

Eyeliner

Mascara

Lashes

Brows

LIPS

Lip color

Lip liner

Lip gloss

OTHER

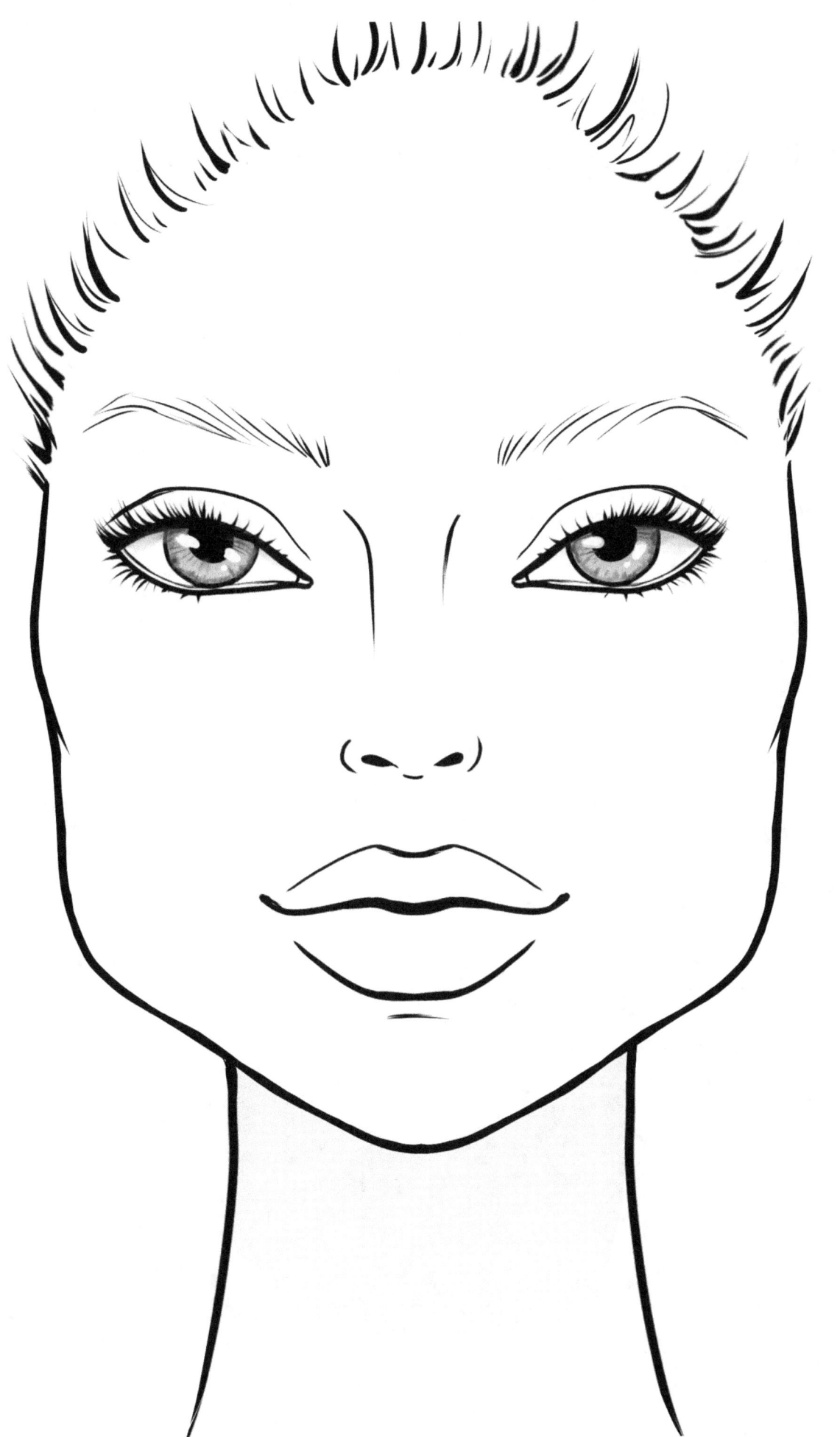

PREPARATION

Cleanser

Moisturizer

Primer

FACE

Concealer

Foundation

Powder

Highlighter

Contour

Bronzer

Blush

EYES

Eyeshadow lid

Eyeshadow crease

Eyeliner

Mascara

Lashes

Brows

LIPS

Lip color

Lip liner

Lip gloss

OTHER

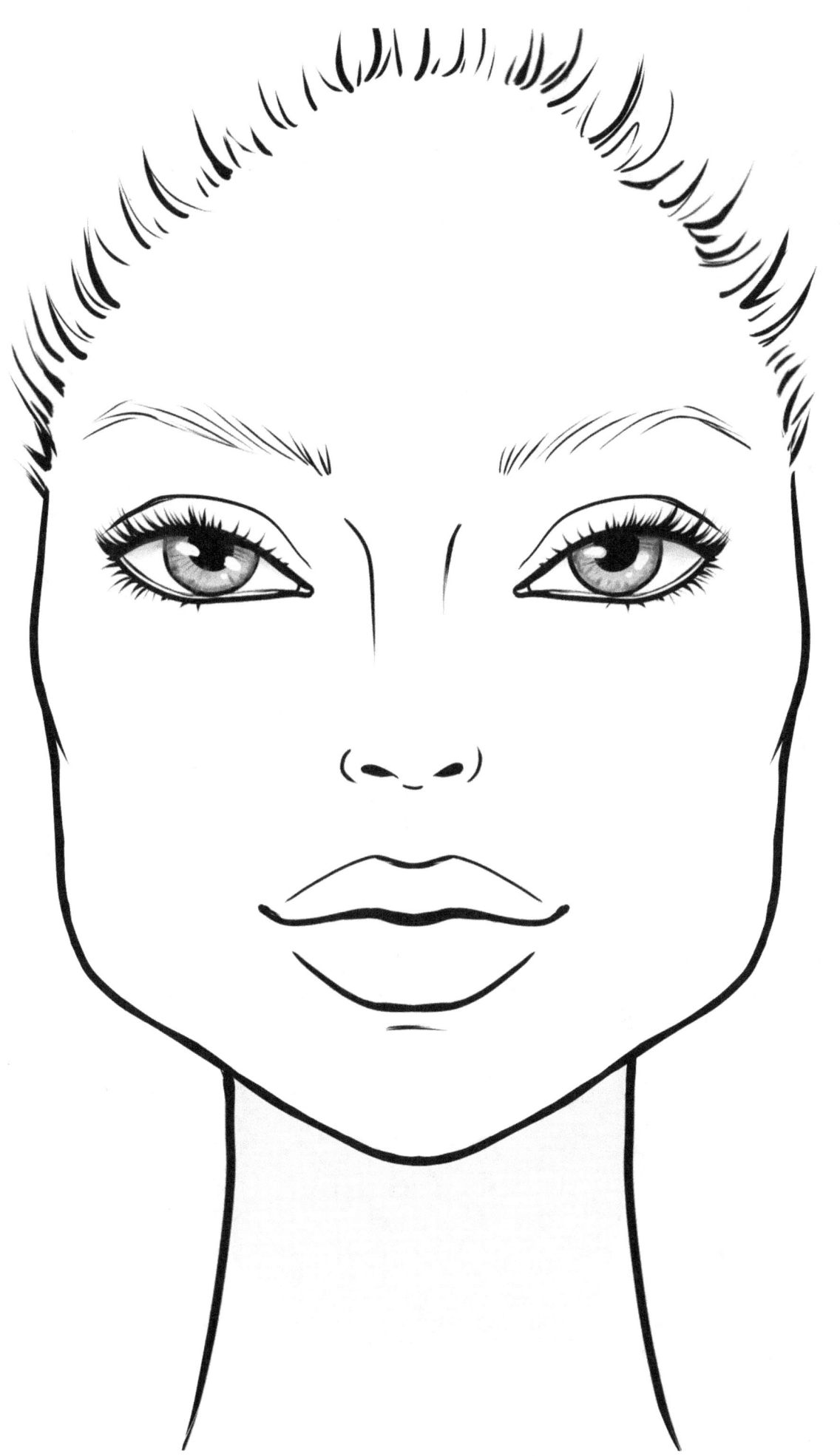

PREPARATION

Cleanser

Moisturizer

Primer

FACE

Concealer

Foundation

Powder

Highlighter

Contour

Bronzer

Blush

EYES

Eyeshadow lid

Eyeshadow crease

Eyeliner

Mascara

Lashes

Brows

LIPS

Lip color

Lip liner

Lip gloss

OTHER

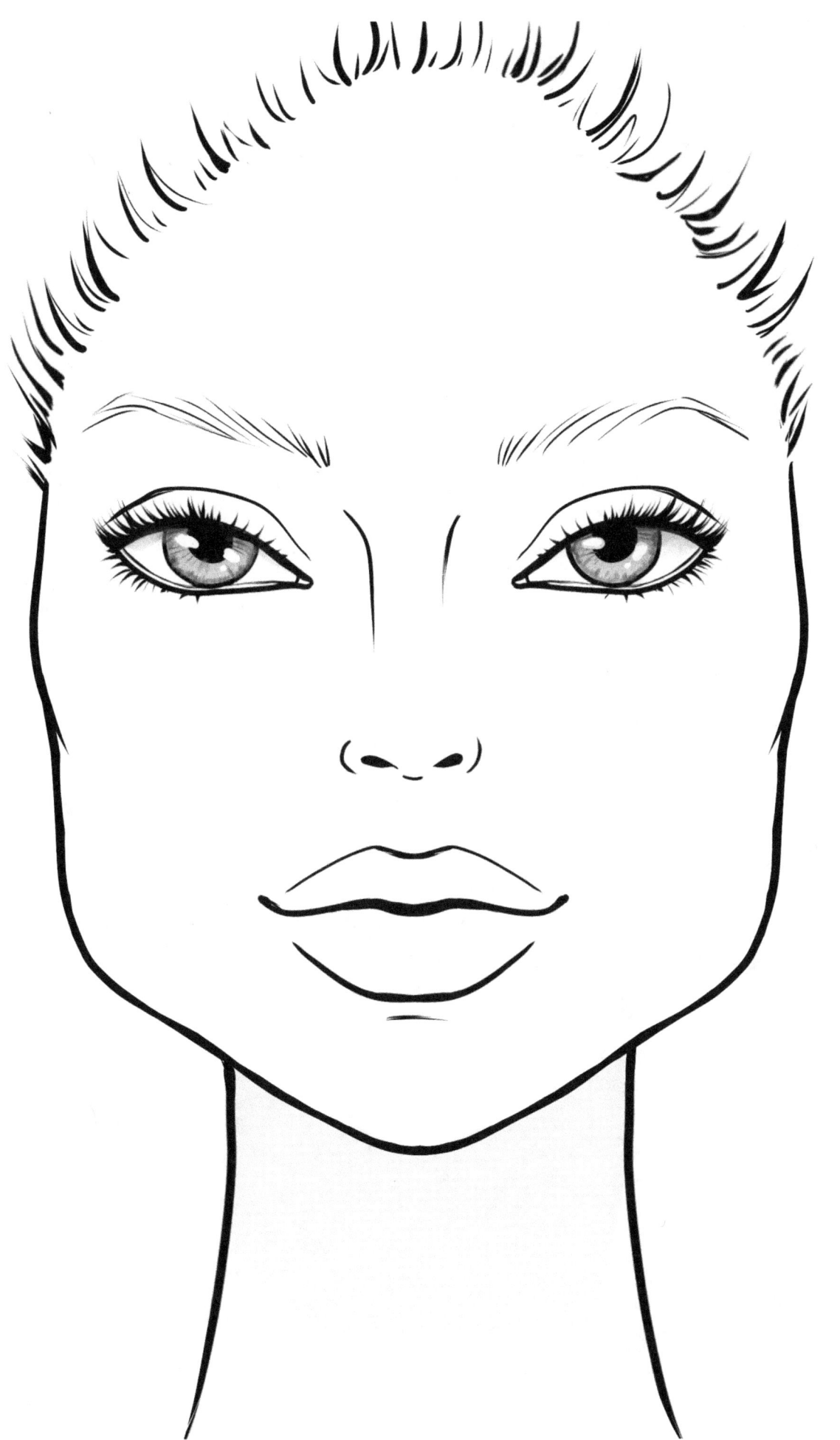

ONE EYE OPENED, ONE EYE CLOSED FACE CHARTS

PREPARATION

Cleanser

Moisturizer

Primer

FACE

Concealer

Foundation

Powder

Highlighter

Contour

Bronzer

Blush

EYES

Eyeshadow lid

Eyeshadow crease

Eyeliner

Mascara

Lashes

Brows

LIPS

Lip color

Lip liner

Lip gloss

OTHER

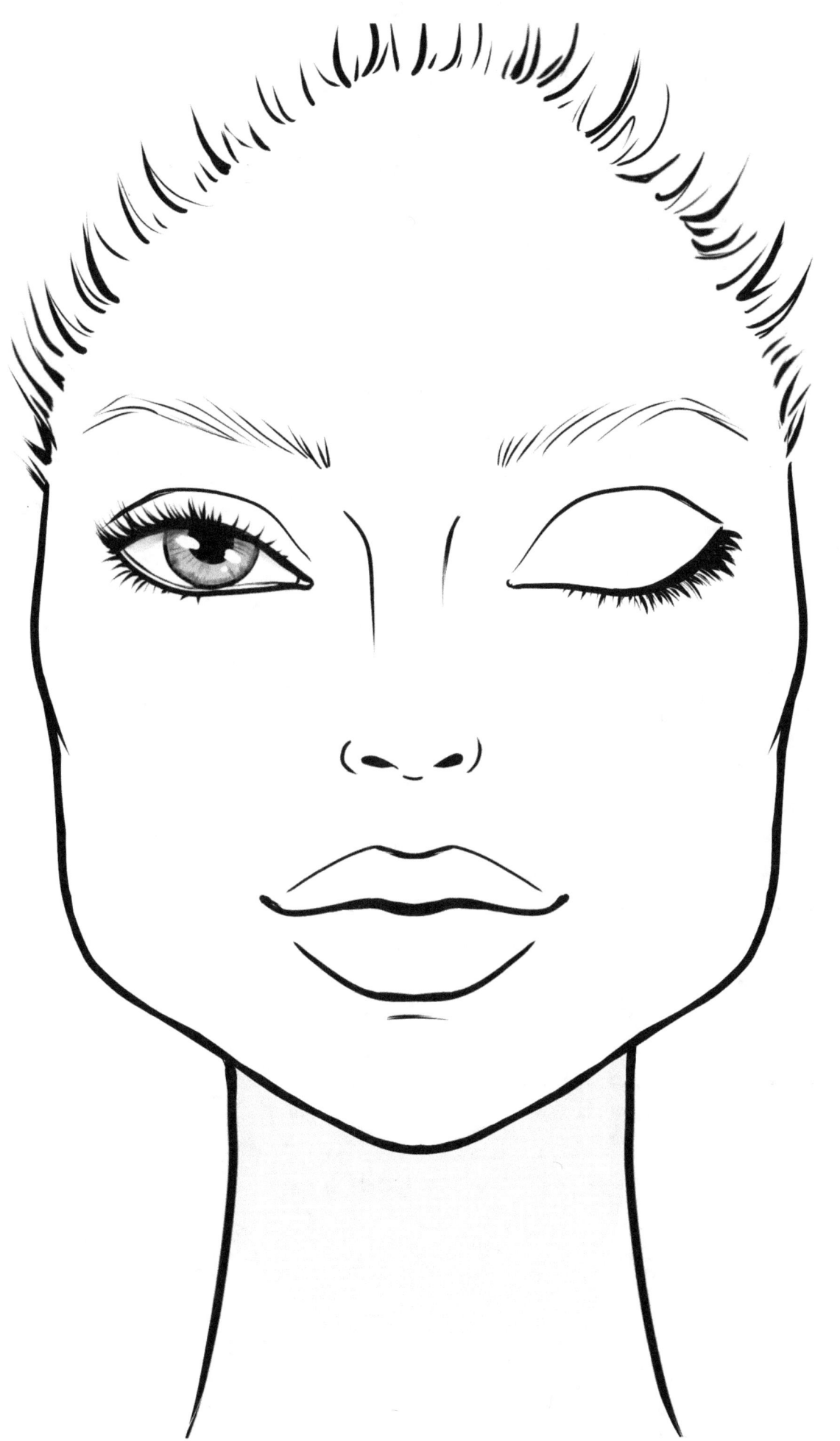

PREPARATION

Cleanser

Moisturizer

Primer

FACE

Concealer

Foundation

Powder

Highlighter

Contour

Bronzer

Blush

EYES

Eyeshadow lid

Eyeshadow crease

Eyeliner

Mascara

Lashes

Brows

LIPS

Lip color

Lip liner

Lip gloss

OTHER

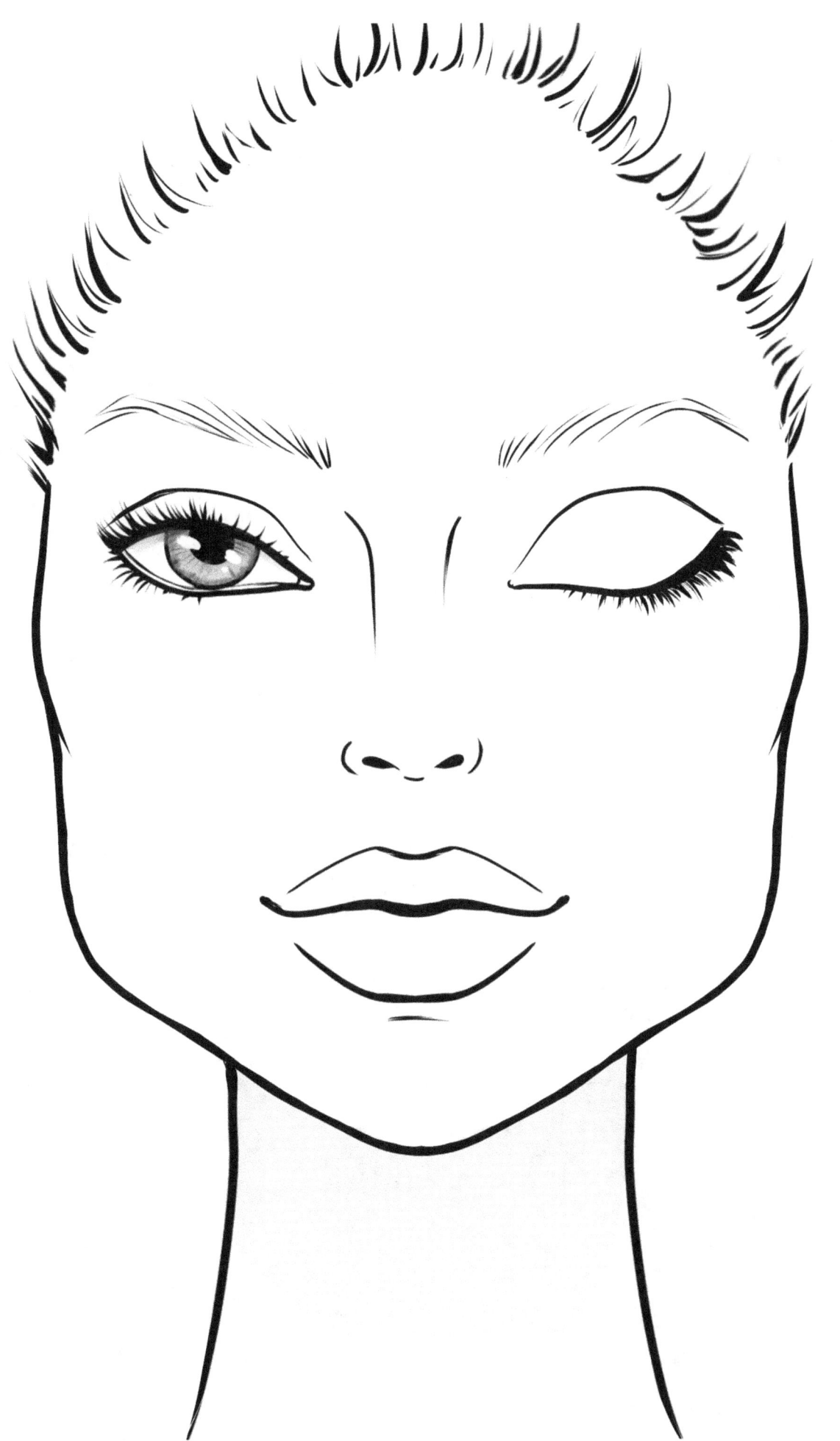

PREPARATION

Cleanser

Moisturizer

Primer

FACE

Concealer

Foundation

Powder

Highlighter

Contour

Bronzer

Blush

EYES

Eyeshadow lid

Eyeshadow crease

Eyeliner

Mascara

Lashes

Brows

LIPS

Lip color

Lip liner

Lip gloss

OTHER

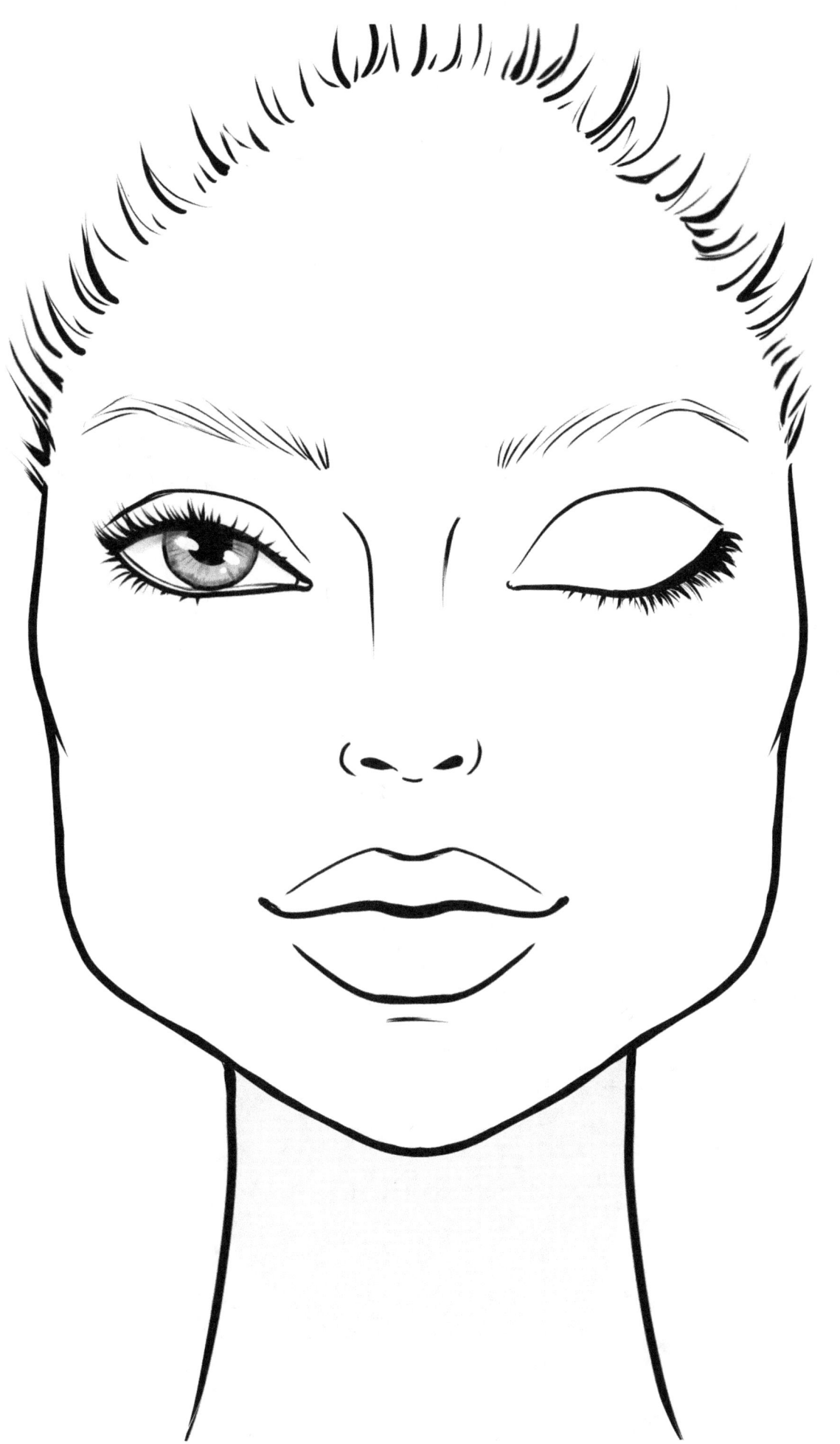

PREPARATION

Cleanser

Moisturizer

Primer

FACE

Concealer

Foundation

Powder

Highlighter

Contour

Bronzer

Blush

EYES

Eyeshadow lid

Eyeshadow crease

Eyeliner

Mascara

Lashes

Brows

LIPS

Lip color

Lip liner

Lip gloss

OTHER

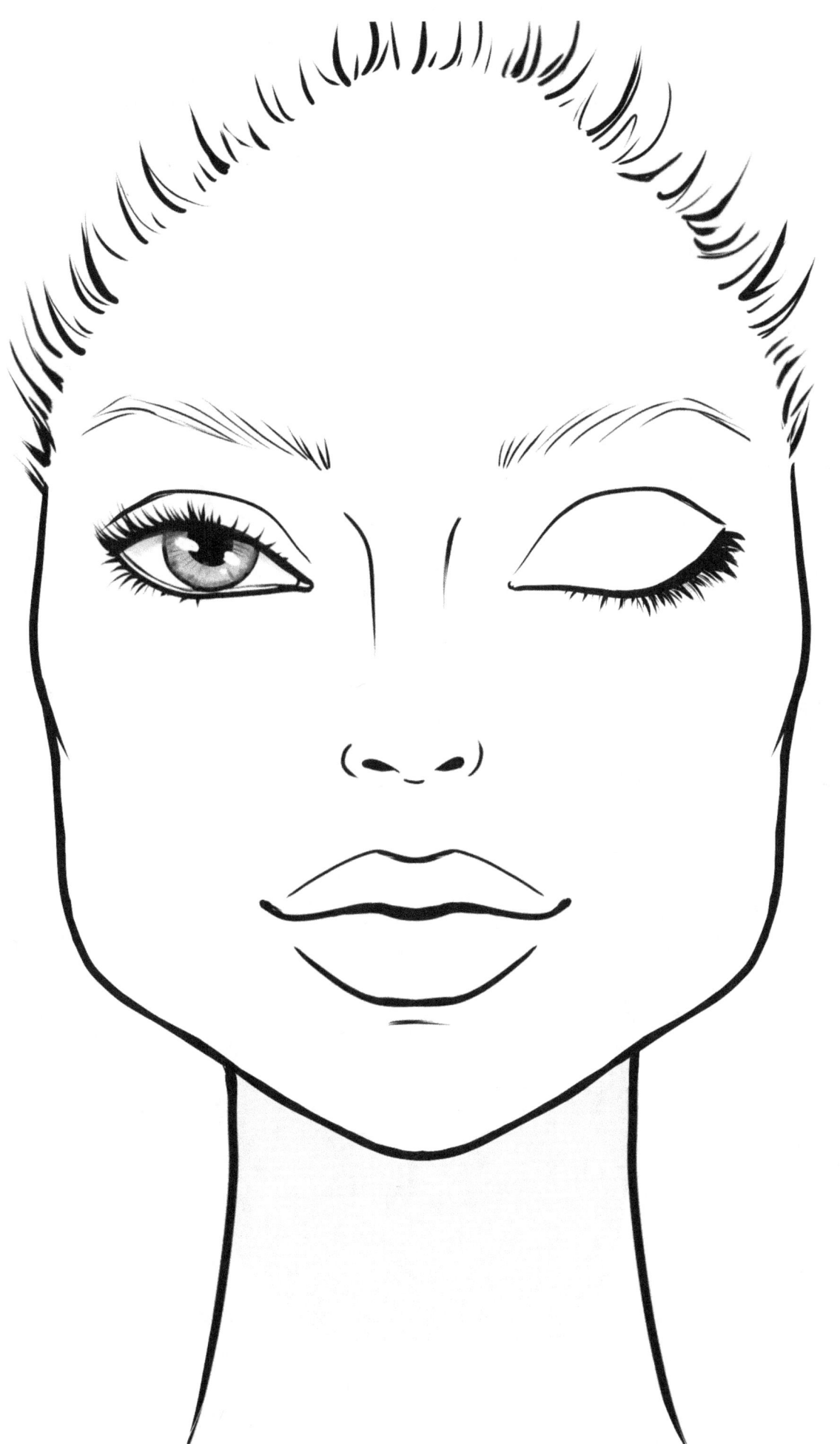

PREPARATION

Cleanser

Moisturizer

Primer

FACE

Concealer

Foundation

Powder

Highlighter

Contour

Bronzer

Blush

EYES

Eyeshadow lid

Eyeshadow crease

Eyeliner

Mascara

Lashes

Brows

LIPS

Lip color

Lip liner

Lip gloss

OTHER

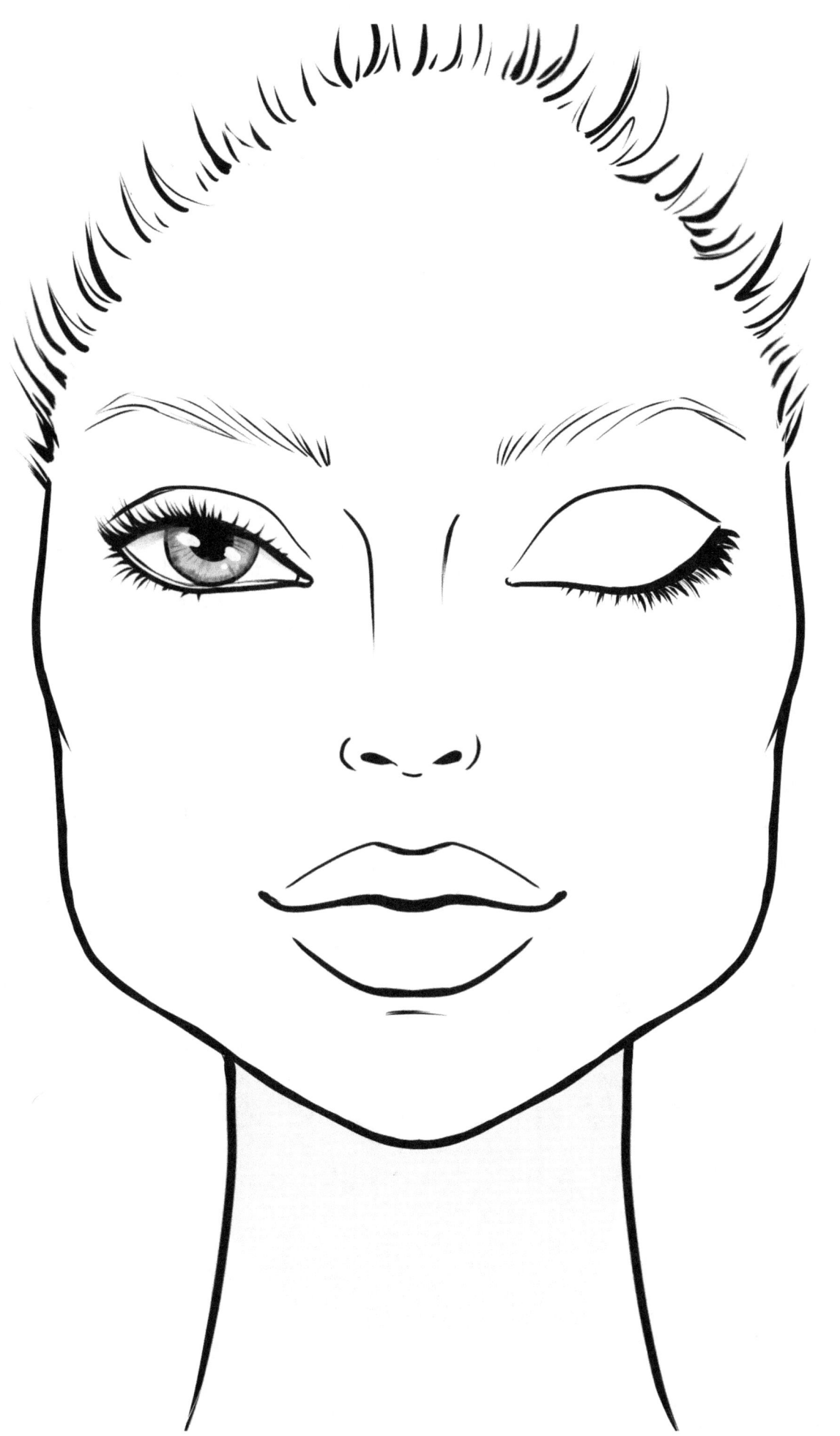

PREPARATION

Cleanser

Moisturizer

Primer

FACE

Concealer

Foundation

Powder

Highlighter

Contour

Bronzer

Blush

EYES

Eyeshadow lid

Eyeshadow crease

Eyeliner

Mascara

Lashes

Brows

LIPS

Lip color

Lip liner

Lip gloss

OTHER

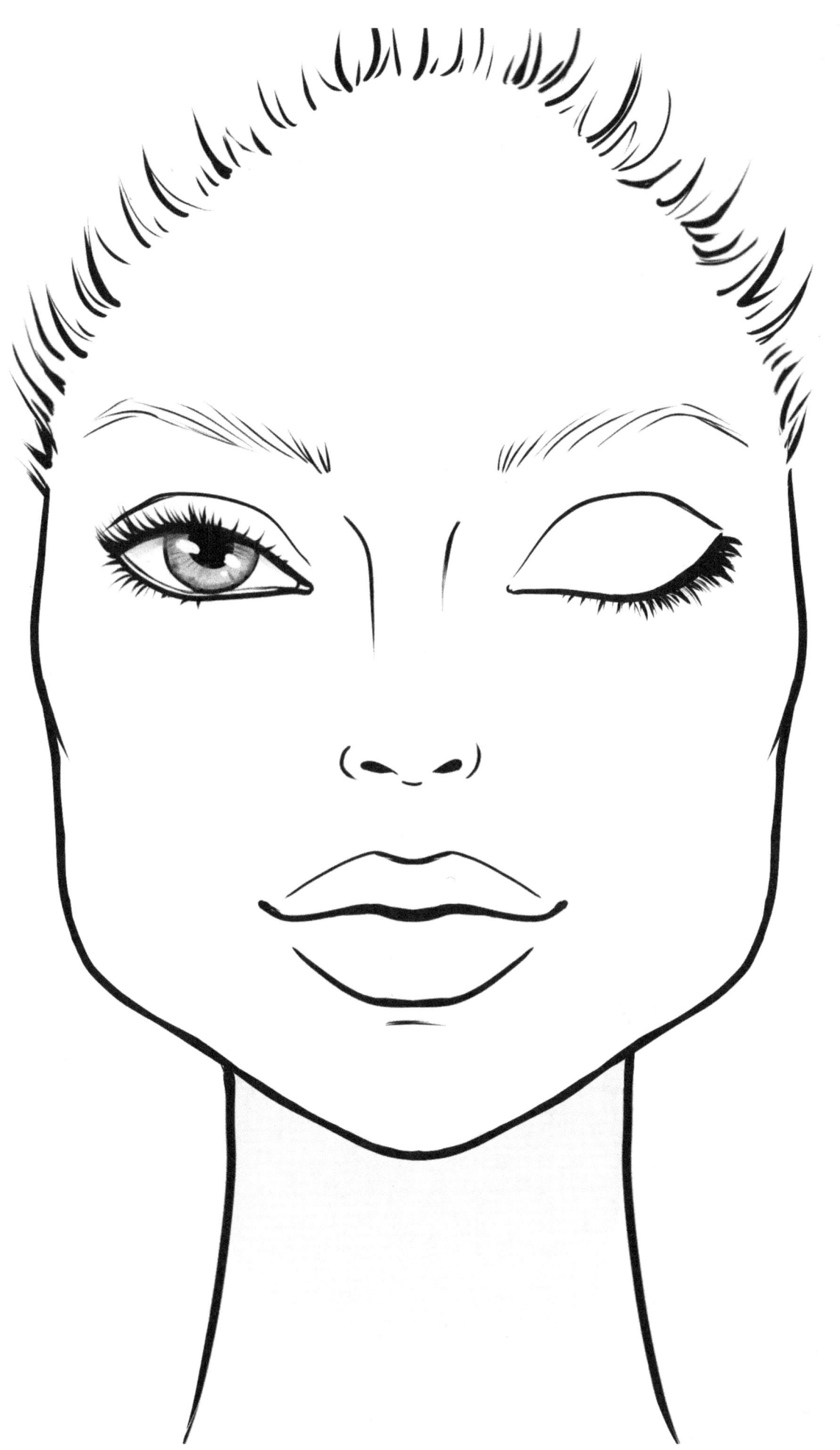

PREPARATION

Cleanser

Moisturizer

Primer

FACE

Concealer

Foundation

Powder

Highlighter

Contour

Bronzer

Blush

EYES

Eyeshadow lid

Eyeshadow crease

Eyeliner

Mascara

Lashes

Brows

LIPS

Lip color

Lip liner

Lip gloss

OTHER

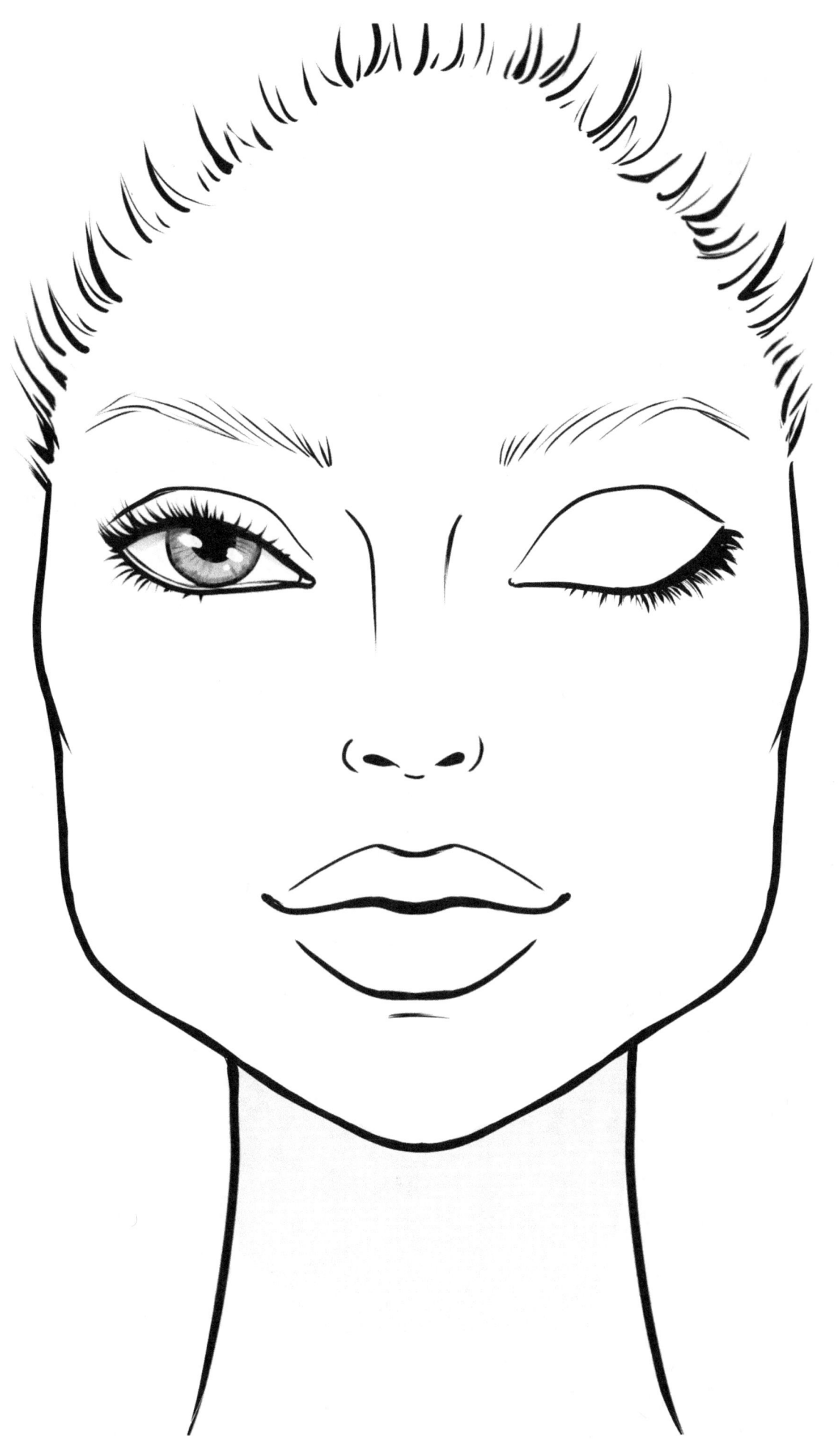

PREPARATION

Cleanser

Moisturizer

Primer

FACE

Concealer

Foundation

Powder

Highlighter

Contour

Bronzer

Blush

EYES

Eyeshadow lid

Eyeshadow crease

Eyeliner

Mascara

Lashes

Brows

LIPS

Lip color

Lip liner

Lip gloss

OTHER

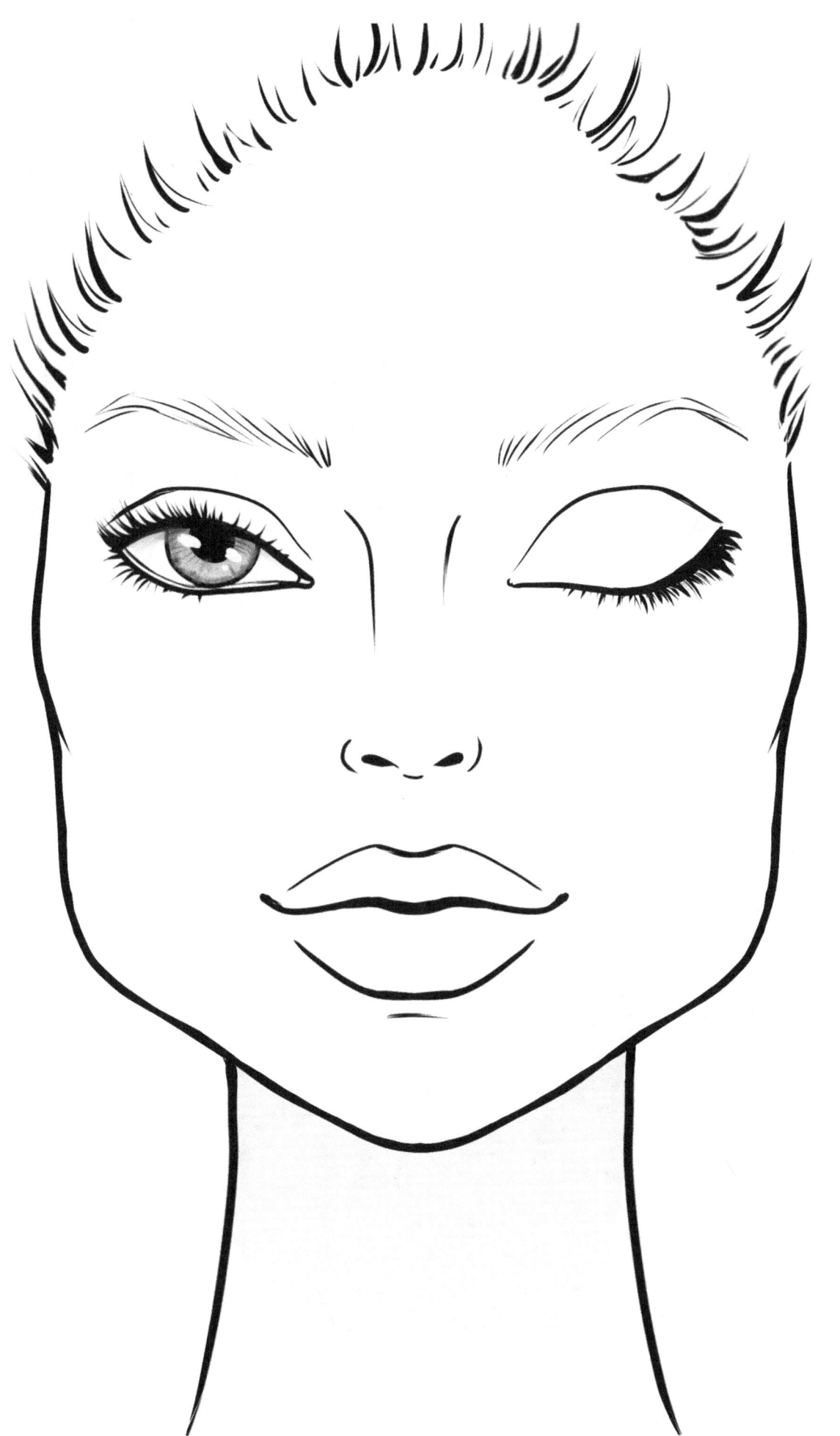

PREPARATION

Cleanser

Moisturizer

Primer

FACE

Concealer

Foundation

Powder

Highlighter

Contour

Bronzer

Blush

EYES

Eyeshadow lid

Eyeshadow crease

Eyeliner

Mascara

Lashes

Brows

LIPS

Lip color

Lip liner

Lip gloss

OTHER

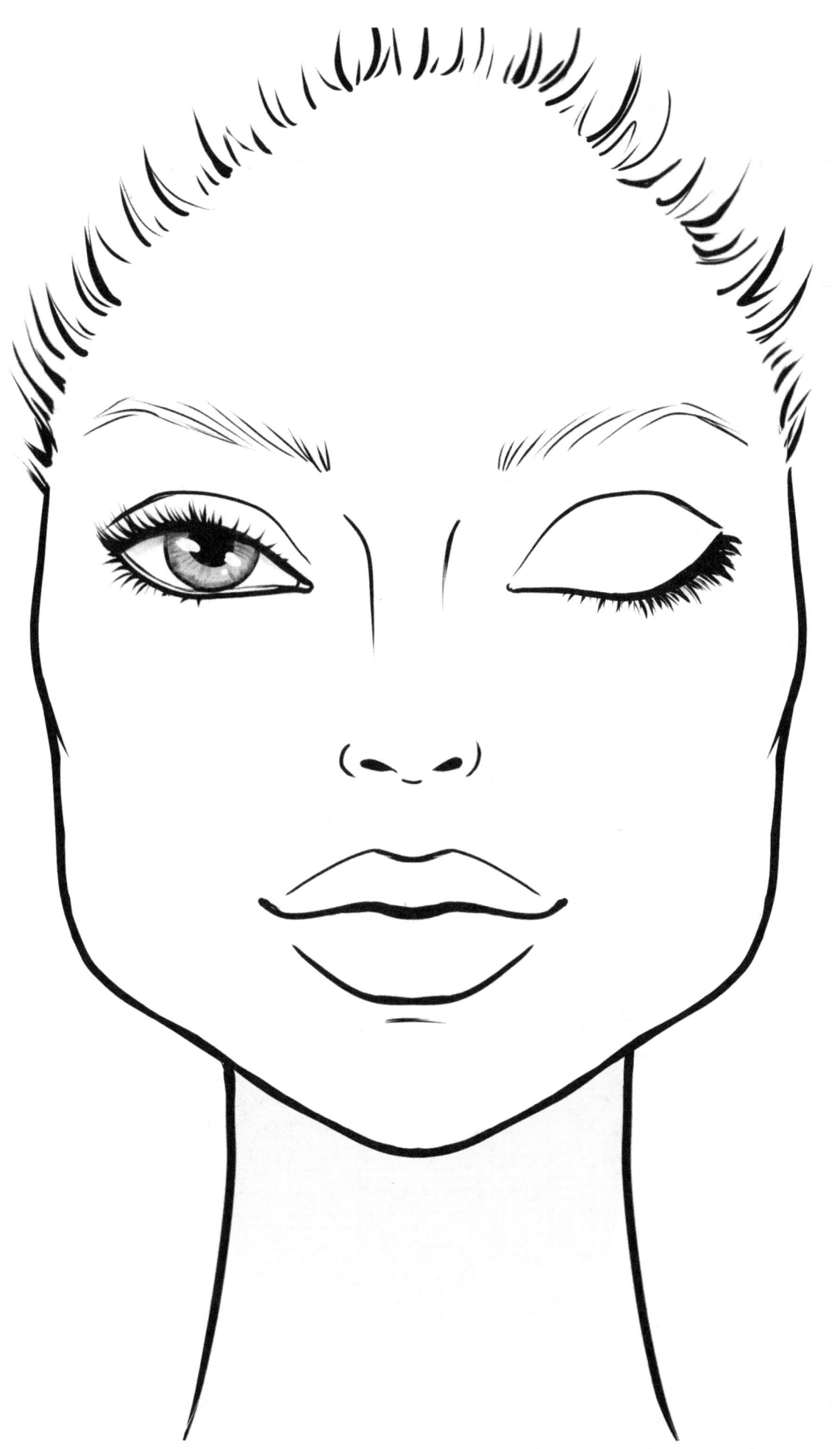

PREPARATION

Cleanser

Moisturizer

Primer

FACE

Concealer

Foundation

Powder

Highlighter

Contour

Bronzer

Blush

EYES

Eyeshadow lid

Eyeshadow crease

Eyeliner

Mascara

Lashes

Brows

LIPS

Lip color

Lip liner

Lip gloss

OTHER

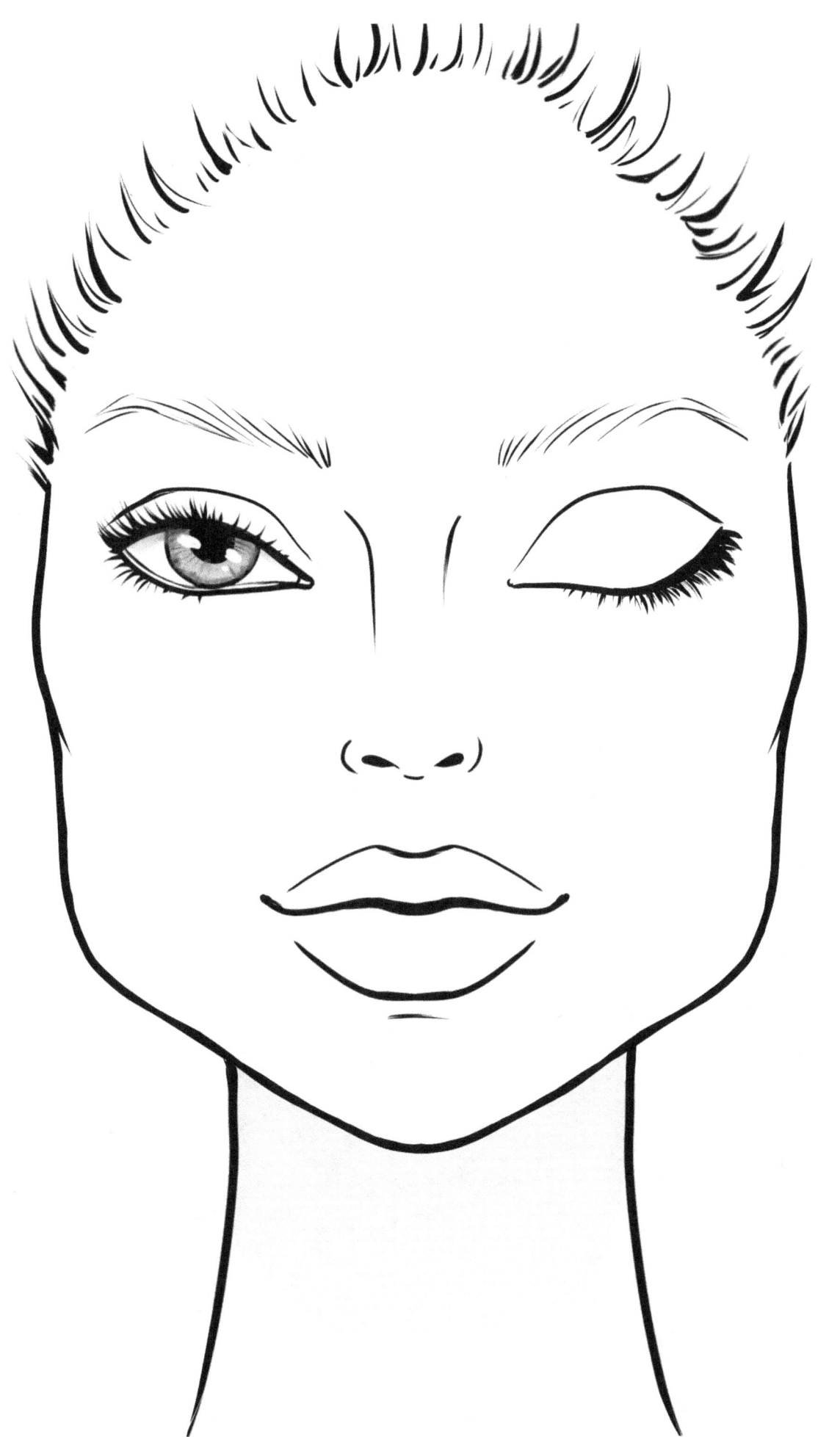

PREPARATION

Cleanser

Moisturizer

Primer

FACE

Concealer

Foundation

Powder

Highlighter

Contour

Bronzer

Blush

EYES

Eyeshadow lid

Eyeshadow crease

Eyeliner

Mascara

Lashes

Brows

LIPS

Lip color

Lip liner

Lip gloss

OTHER

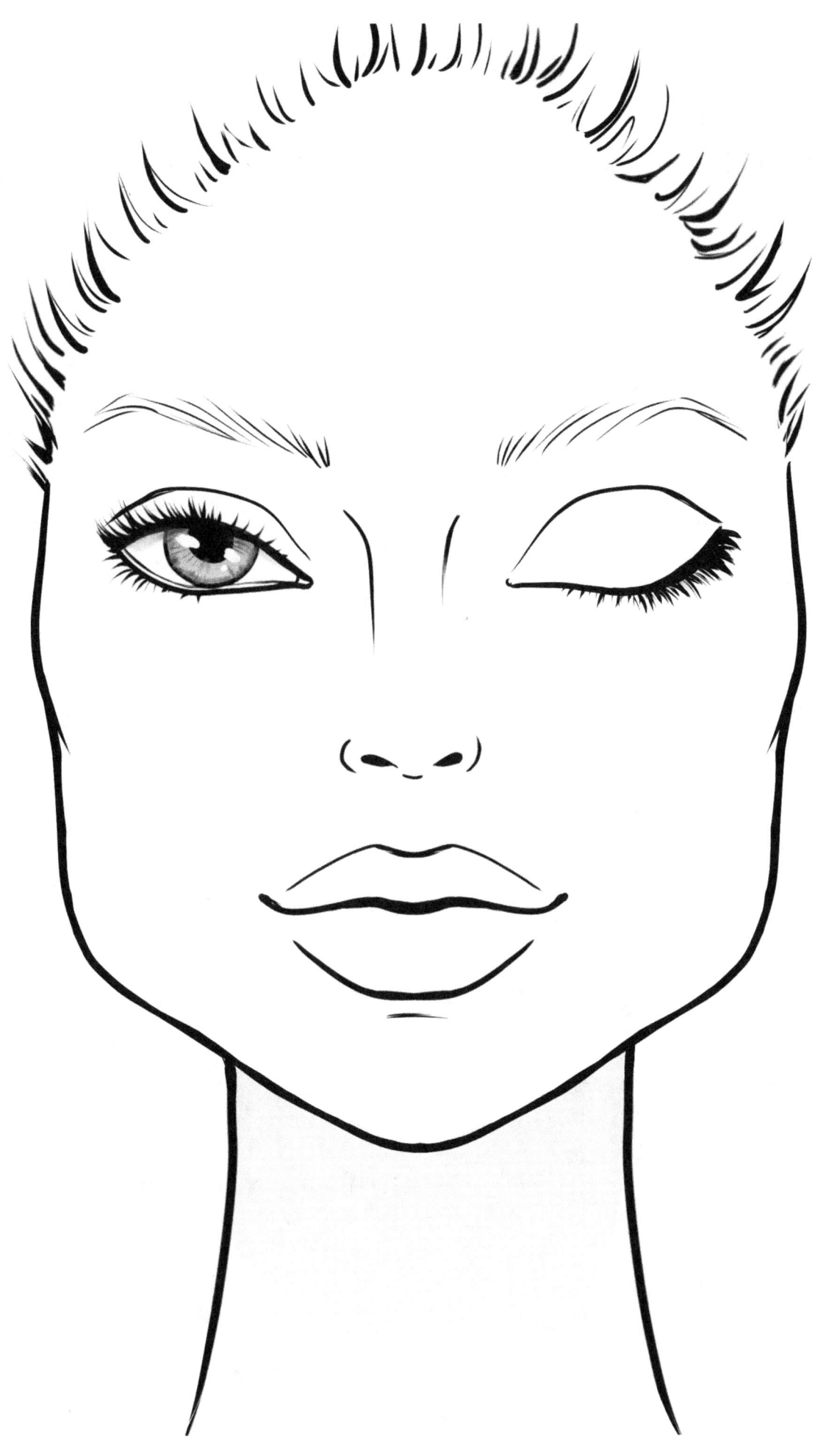

PREPARATION

Cleanser

Moisturizer

Primer

FACE

Concealer

Foundation

Powder

Highlighter

Contour

Bronzer

Blush

EYES

Eyeshadow lid

Eyeshadow crease

Eyeliner

Mascara

Lashes

Brows

LIPS

Lip color

Lip liner

Lip gloss

OTHER

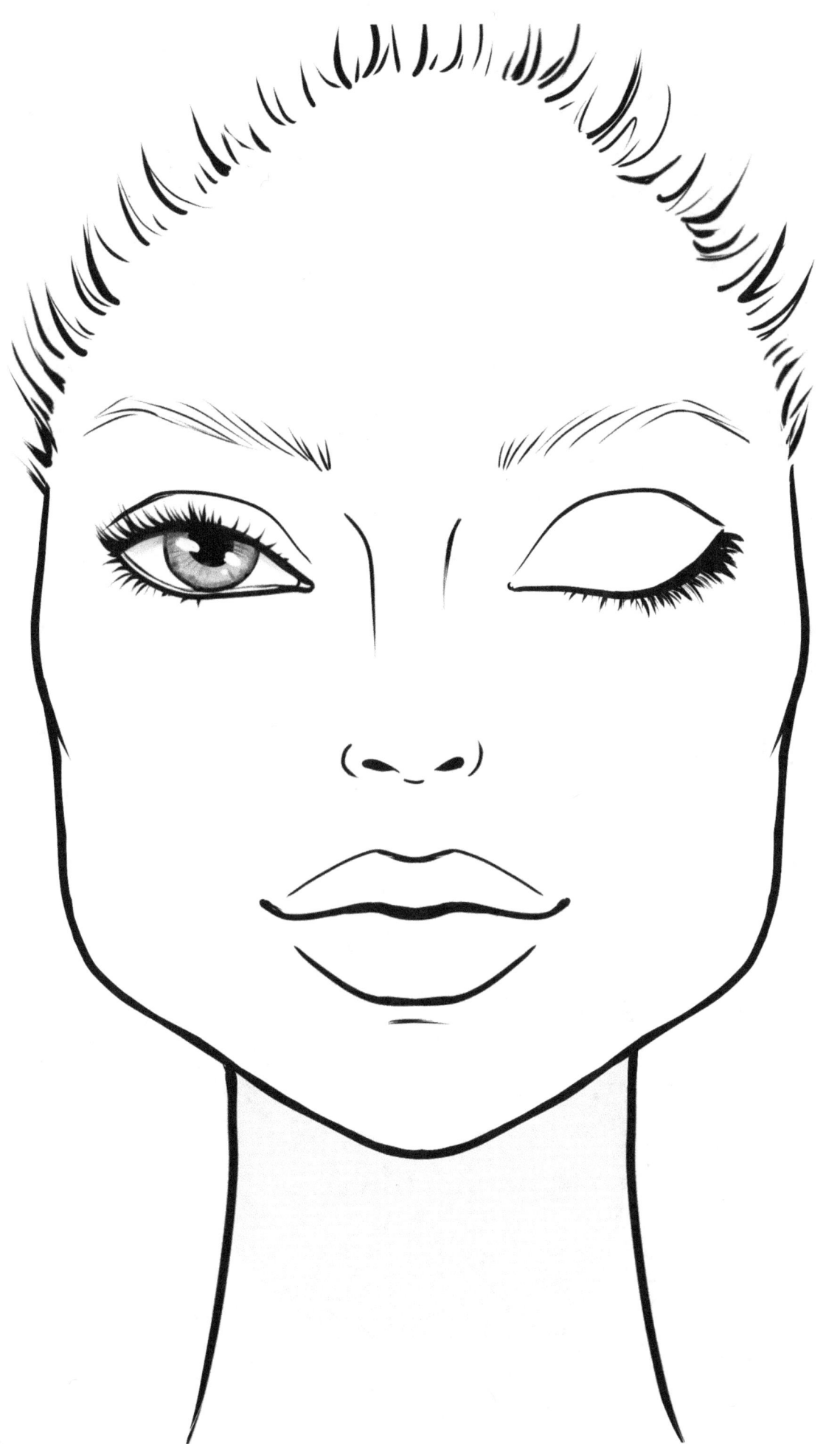

PREPARATION

Cleanser

Moisturizer

Primer

FACE

Concealer

Foundation

Powder

Highlighter

Contour

Bronzer

Blush

EYES

Eyeshadow lid

Eyeshadow crease

Eyeliner

Mascara

Lashes

Brows

LIPS

Lip color

Lip liner

Lip gloss

OTHER

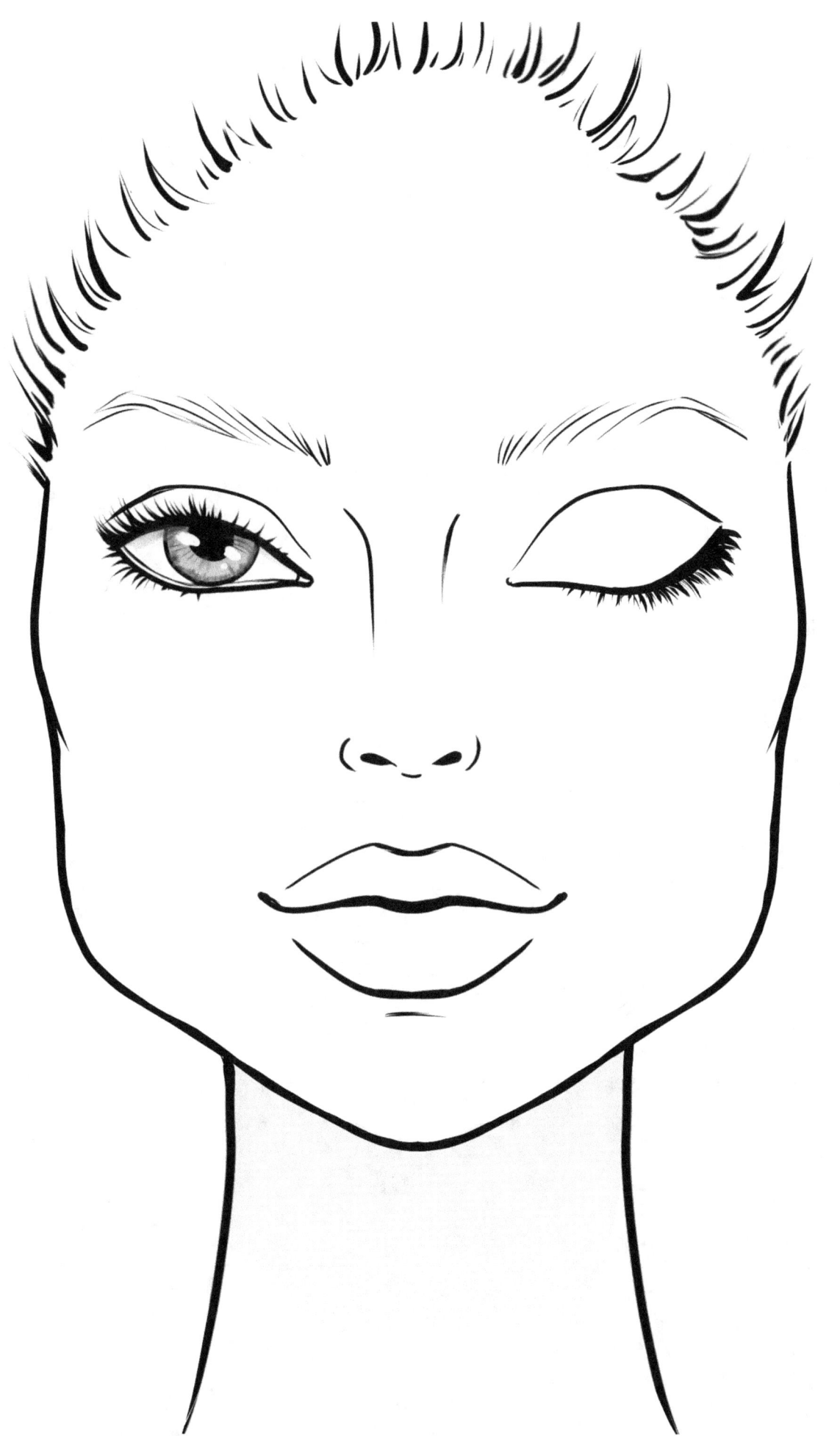

PREPARATION

Cleanser

Moisturizer

Primer

FACE

Concealer

Foundation

Powder

Highlighter

Contour

Bronzer

Blush

EYES

Eyeshadow lid

Eyeshadow crease

Eyeliner

Mascara

Lashes

Brows

LIPS

Lip color

Lip liner

Lip gloss

OTHER

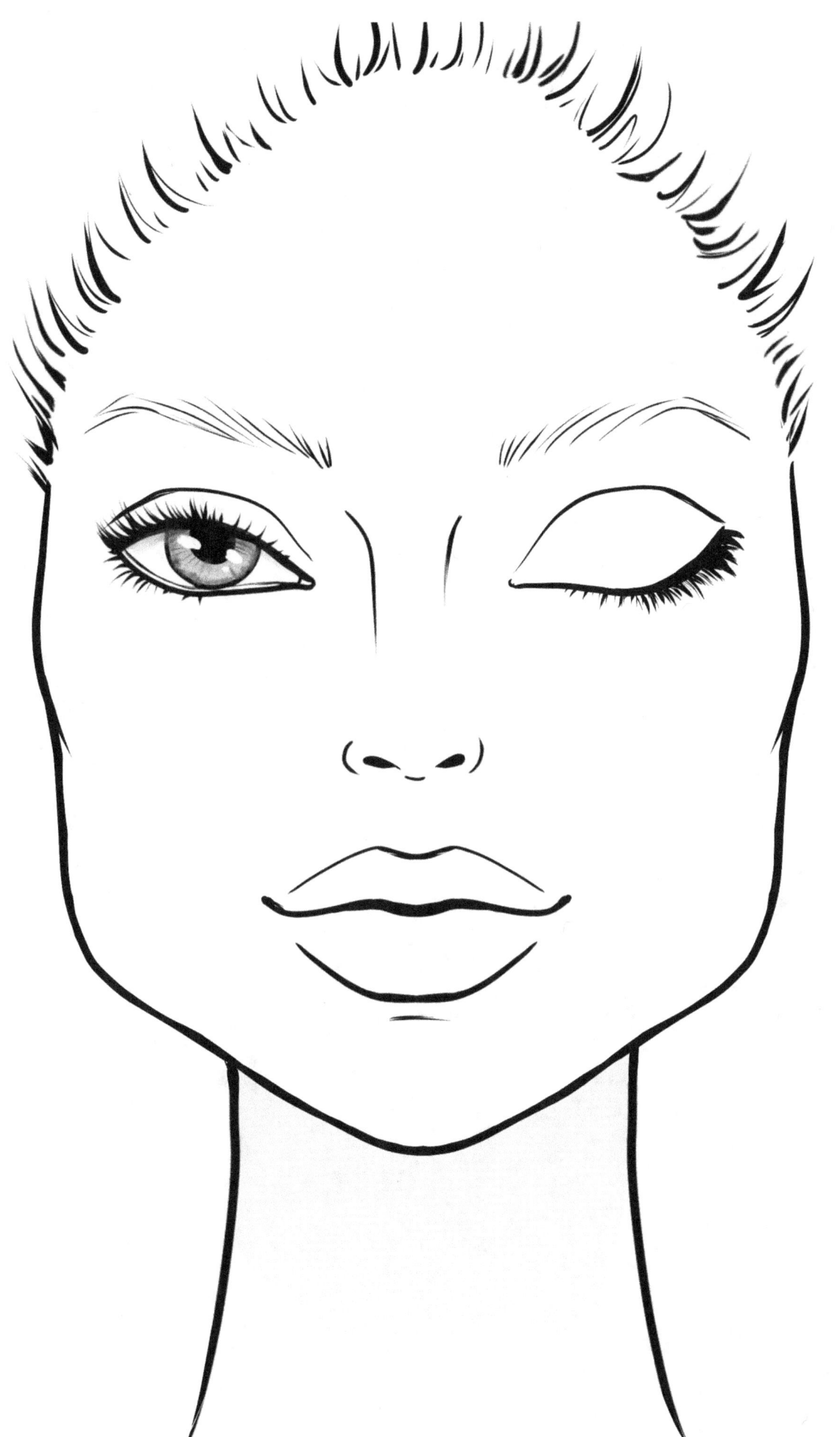

PREPARATION

Cleanser

Moisturizer

Primer

FACE

Concealer

Foundation

Powder

Highlighter

Contour

Bronzer

Blush

EYES

Eyeshadow lid

Eyeshadow crease

Eyeliner

Mascara

Lashes

Brows

LIPS

Lip color

Lip liner

Lip gloss

OTHER

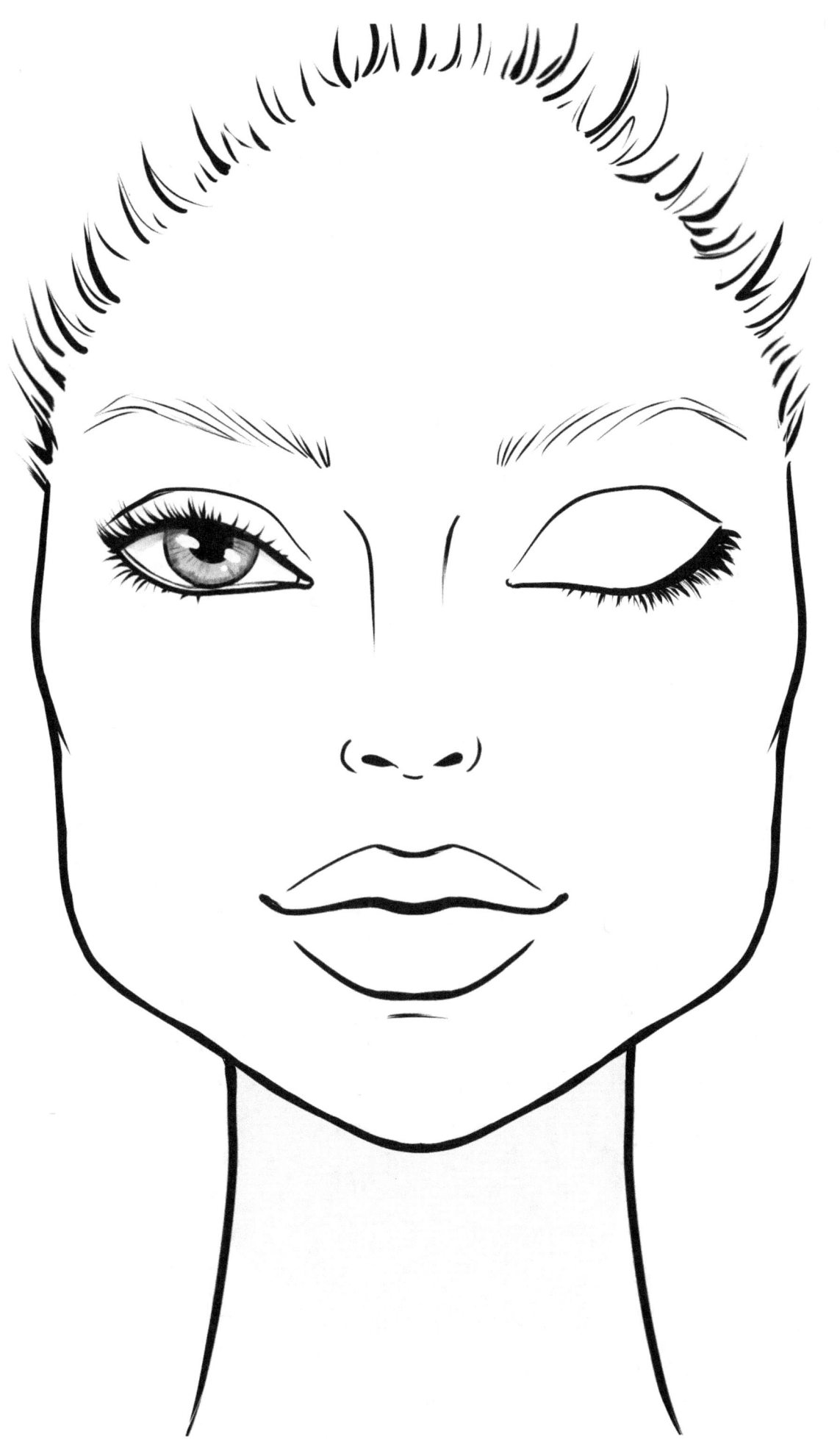

PREPARATION

Cleanser

Moisturizer

Primer

FACE

Concealer

Foundation

Powder

Highlighter

Contour

Bronzer

Blush

EYES

Eyeshadow lid

Eyeshadow crease

Eyeliner

Mascara

Lashes

Brows

LIPS

Lip color

Lip liner

Lip gloss

OTHER

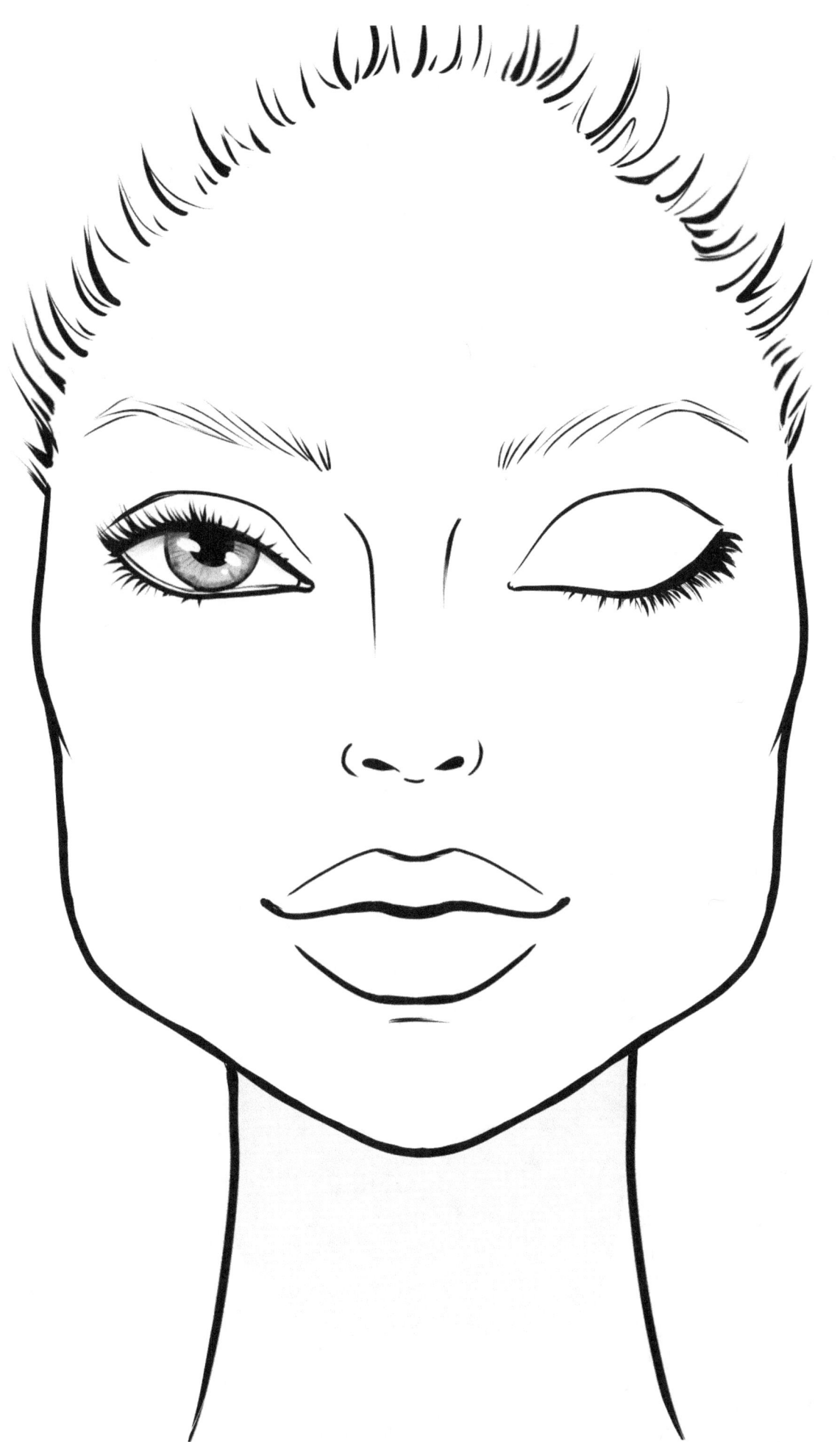

PREPARATION

Cleanser

Moisturizer

Primer

FACE

Concealer

Foundation

Powder

Highlighter

Contour

Bronzer

Blush

EYES

Eyeshadow lid

Eyeshadow crease

Eyeliner

Mascara

Lashes

Brows

LIPS

Lip color

Lip liner

Lip gloss

OTHER

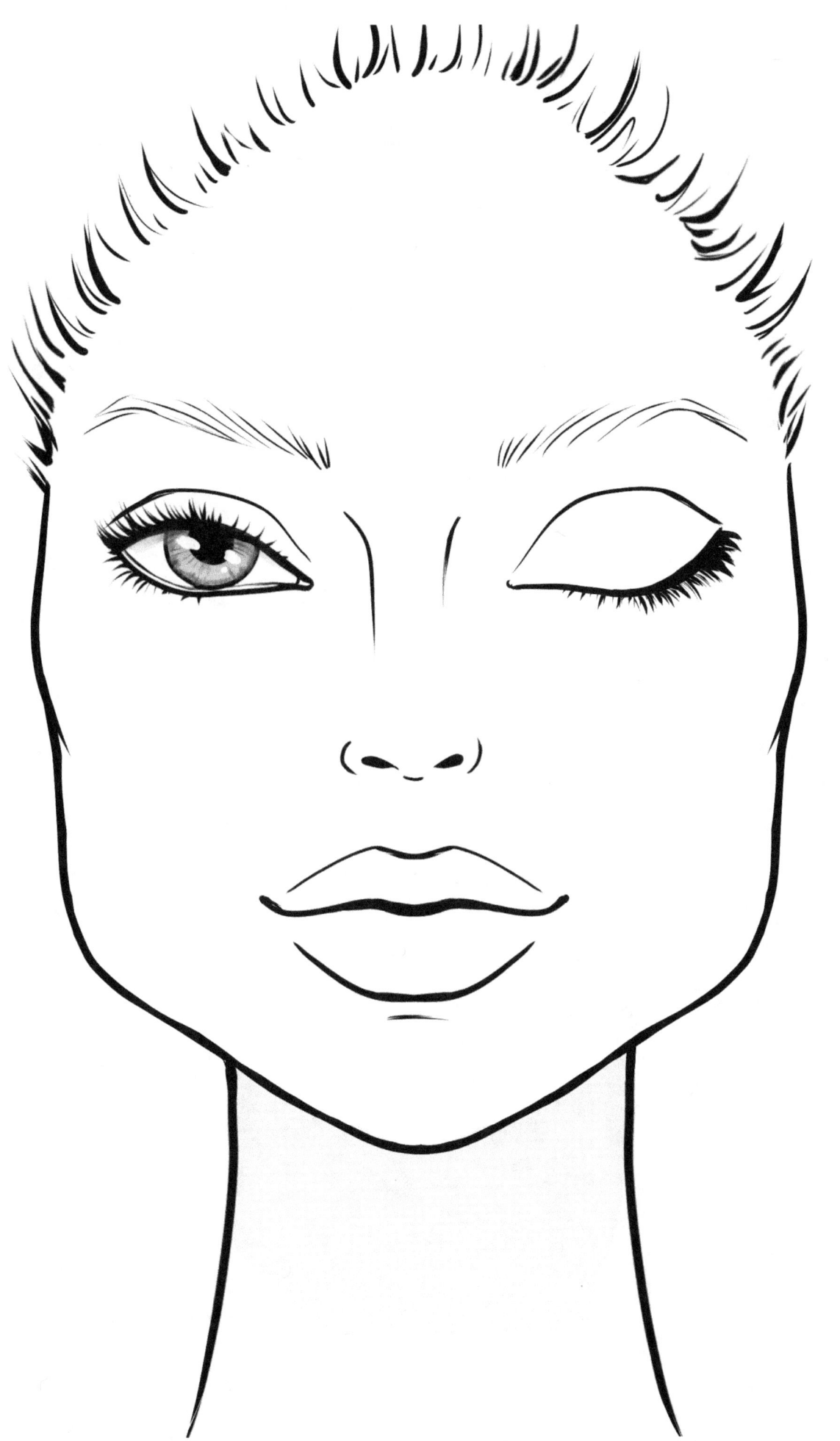

PREPARATION

Cleanser

Moisturizer

Primer

FACE

Concealer

Foundation

Powder

Highlighter

Contour

Bronzer

Blush

EYES

Eyeshadow lid

Eyeshadow crease

Eyeliner

Mascara

Lashes

Brows

LIPS

Lip color

Lip liner

Lip gloss

OTHER

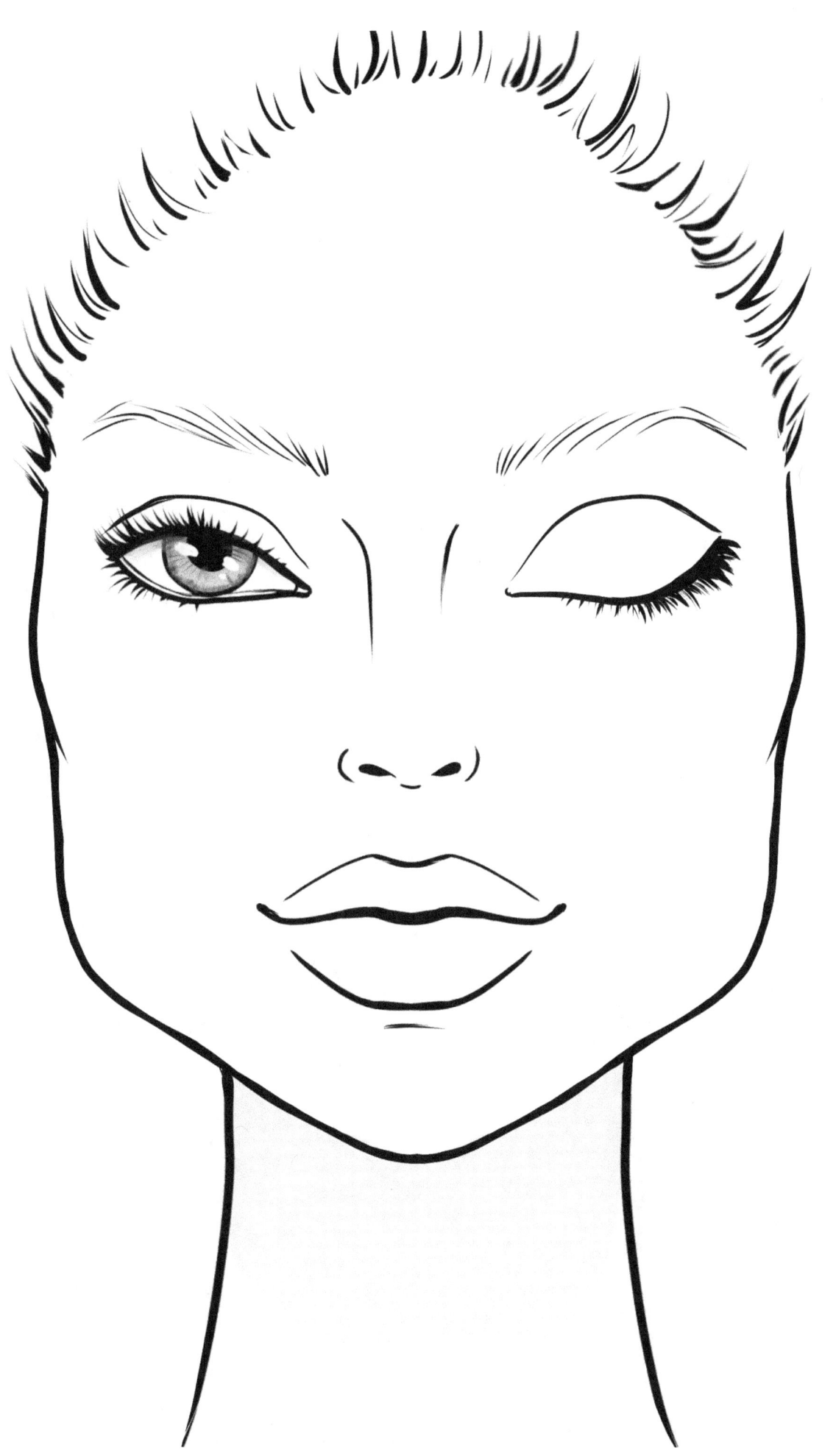

CLOSED EYES
FACE CHARTS

PREPARATION

Cleanser

Moisturizer

Primer

FACE

Concealer

Foundation

Powder

Highlighter

Contour

Bronzer

Blush

EYES

Eyeshadow lid

Eyeshadow crease

Eyeliner

Mascara

Lashes

Brows

LIPS

Lip color

Lip liner

Lip gloss

OTHER

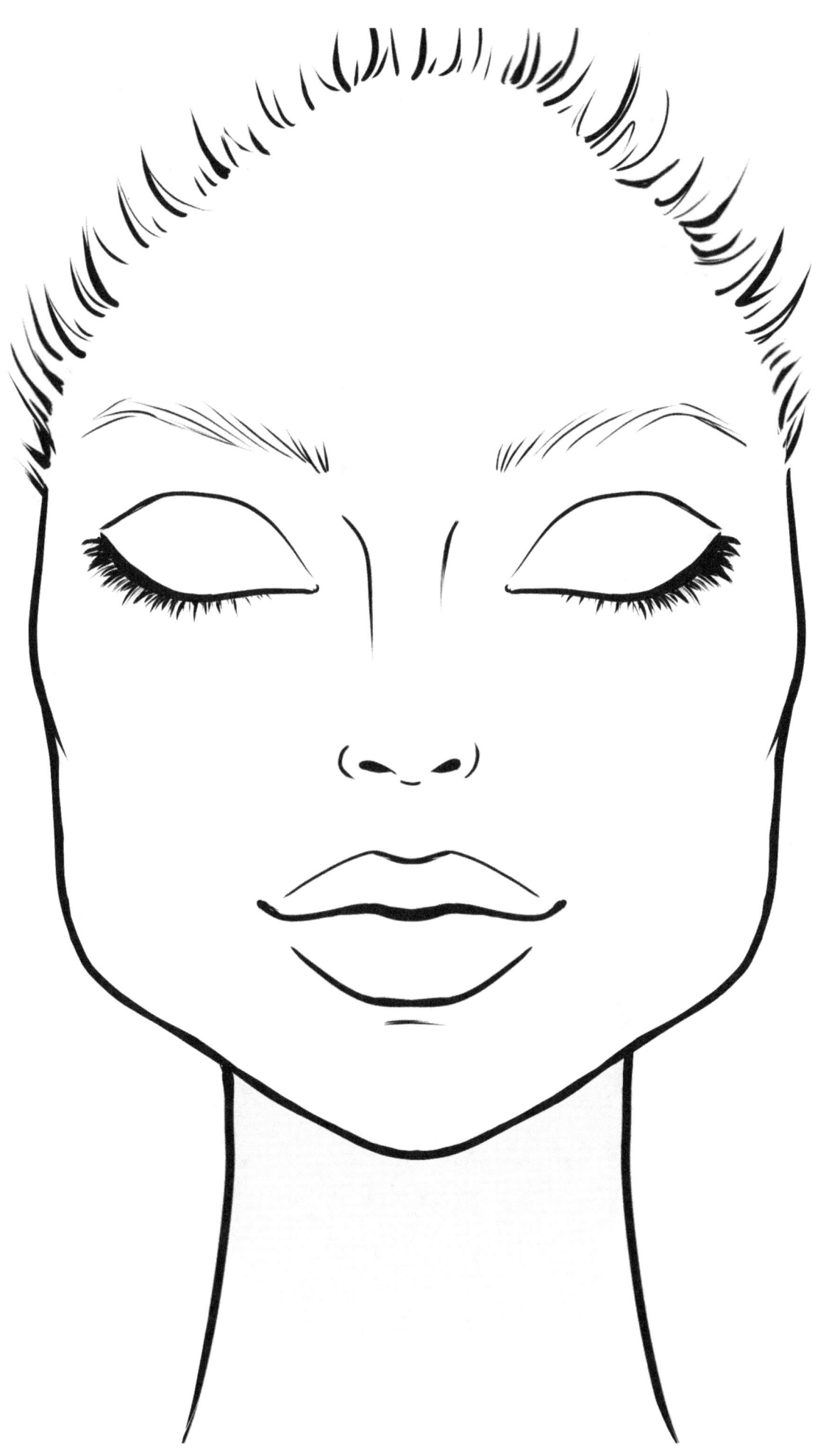

PREPARATION

Cleanser

Moisturizer

Primer

FACE

Concealer

Foundation

Powder

Highlighter

Contour

Bronzer

Blush

EYES

Eyeshadow lid

Eyeshadow crease

Eyeliner

Mascara

Lashes

Brows

LIPS

Lip color

Lip liner

Lip gloss

OTHER

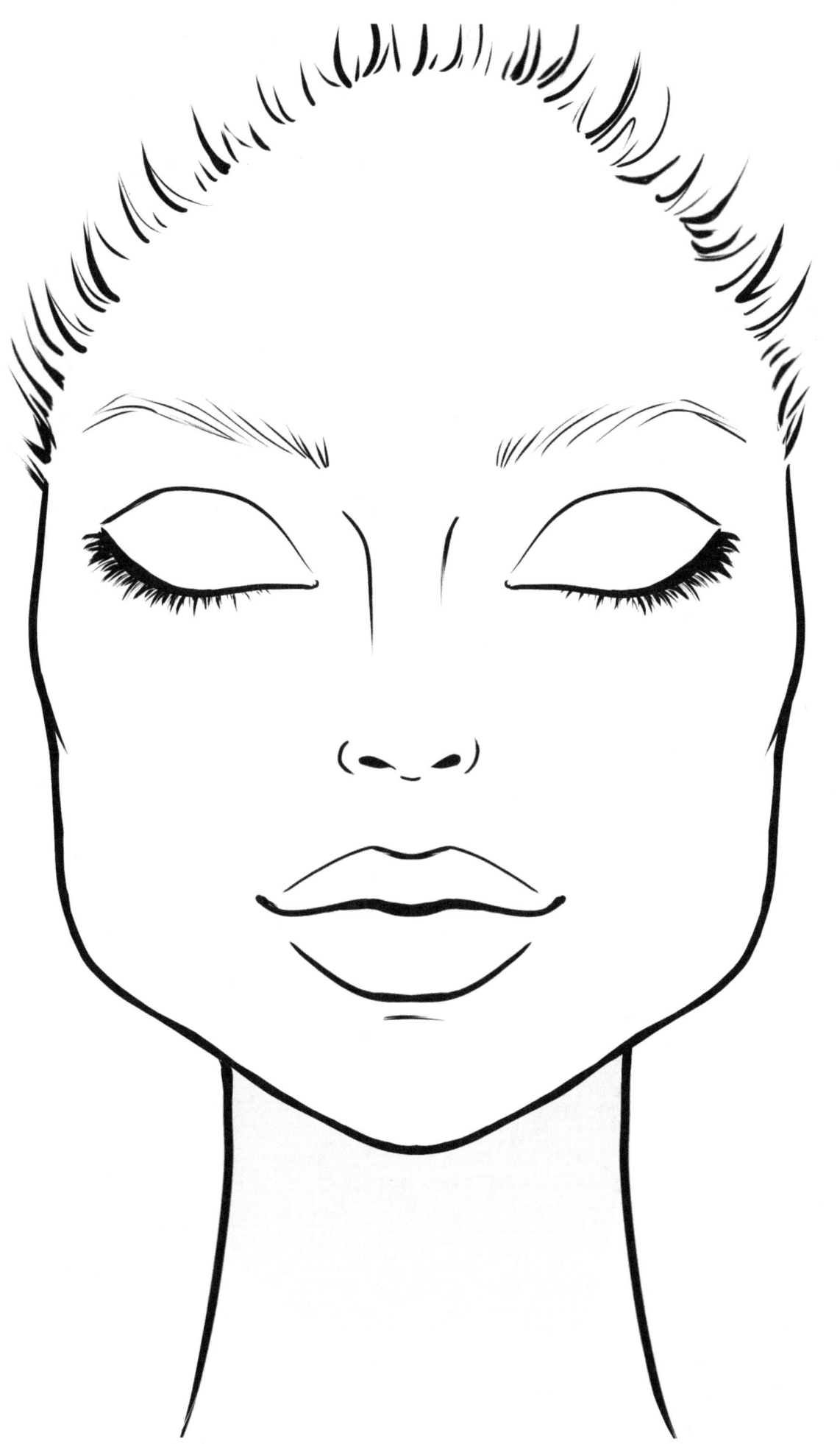

PREPARATION

Cleanser

Moisturizer

Primer

FACE

Concealer

Foundation

Powder

Highlighter

Contour

Bronzer

Blush

EYES

Eyeshadow lid

Eyeshadow crease

Eyeliner

Mascara

Lashes

Brows

LIPS

Lip color

Lip liner

Lip gloss

OTHER

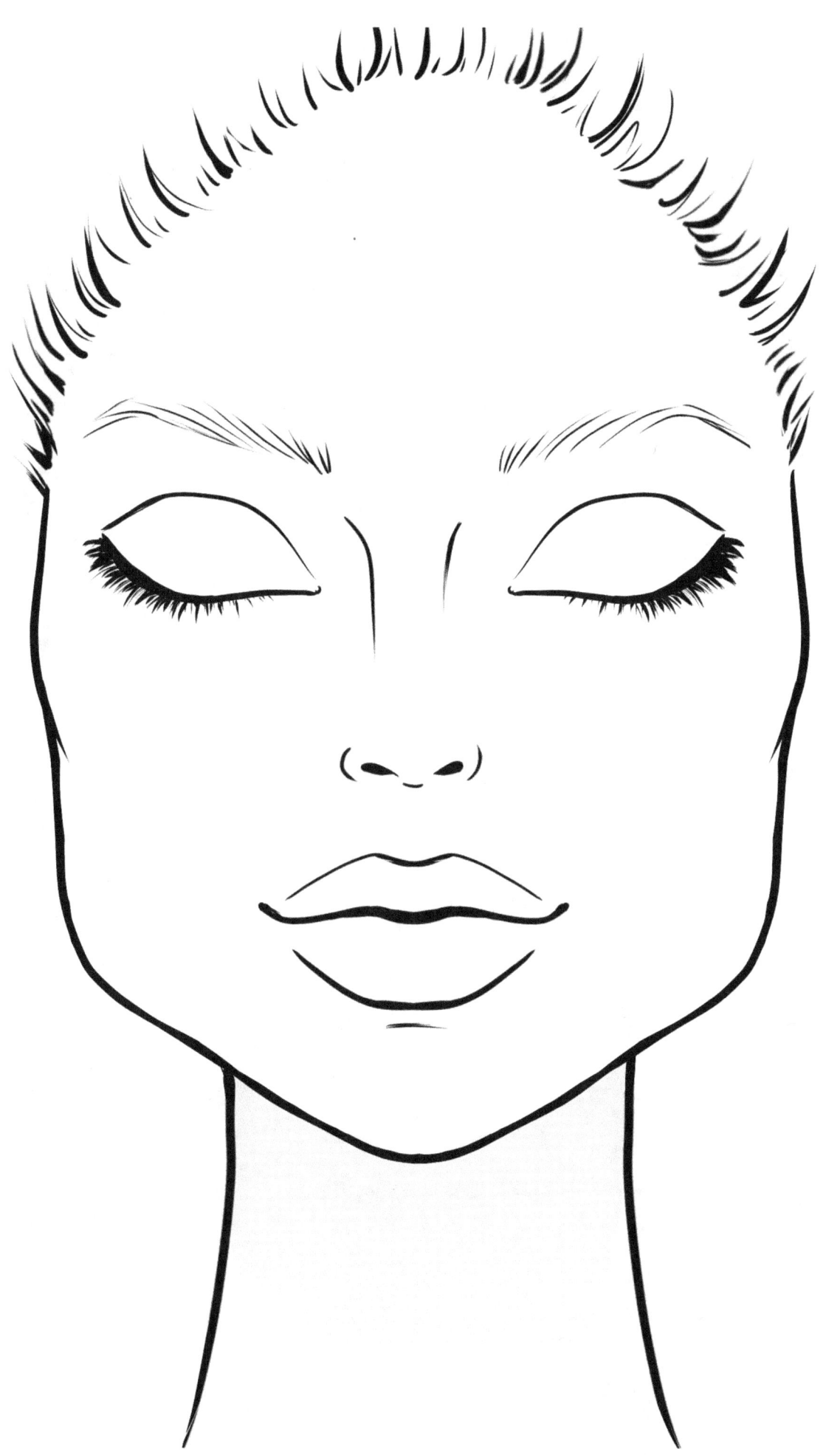

PREPARATION

Cleanser

Moisturizer

Primer

FACE

Concealer

Foundation

Powder

Highlighter

Contour

Bronzer

Blush

EYES

Eyeshadow lid

Eyeshadow crease

Eyeliner

Mascara

Lashes

Brows

LIPS

Lip color

Lip liner

Lip gloss

OTHER

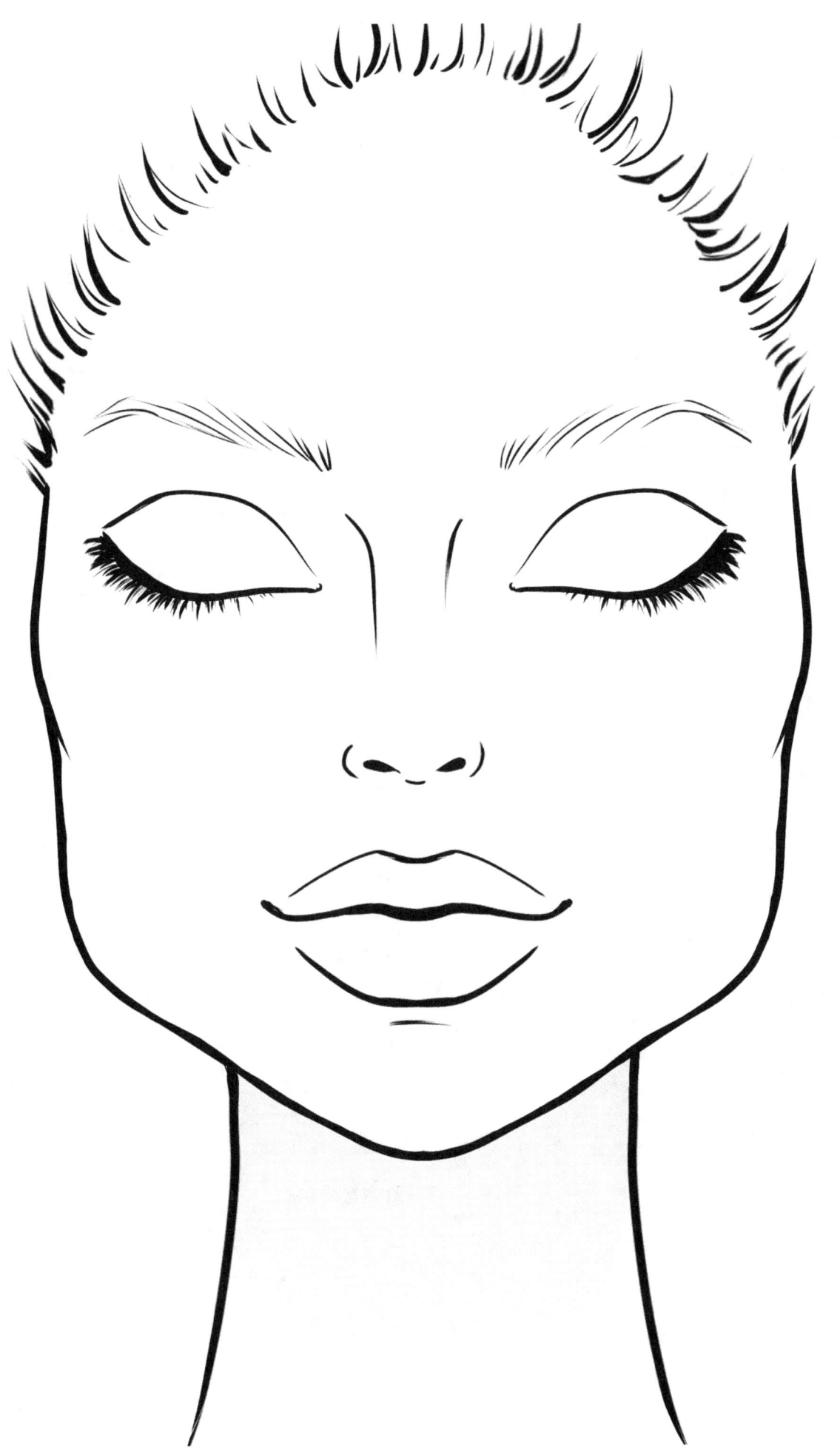

PREPARATION

Cleanser

Moisturizer

Primer

FACE

Concealer

Foundation

Powder

Highlighter

Contour

Bronzer

Blush

EYES

Eyeshadow lid

Eyeshadow crease

Eyeliner

Mascara

Lashes

Brows

LIPS

Lip color

Lip liner

Lip gloss

OTHER

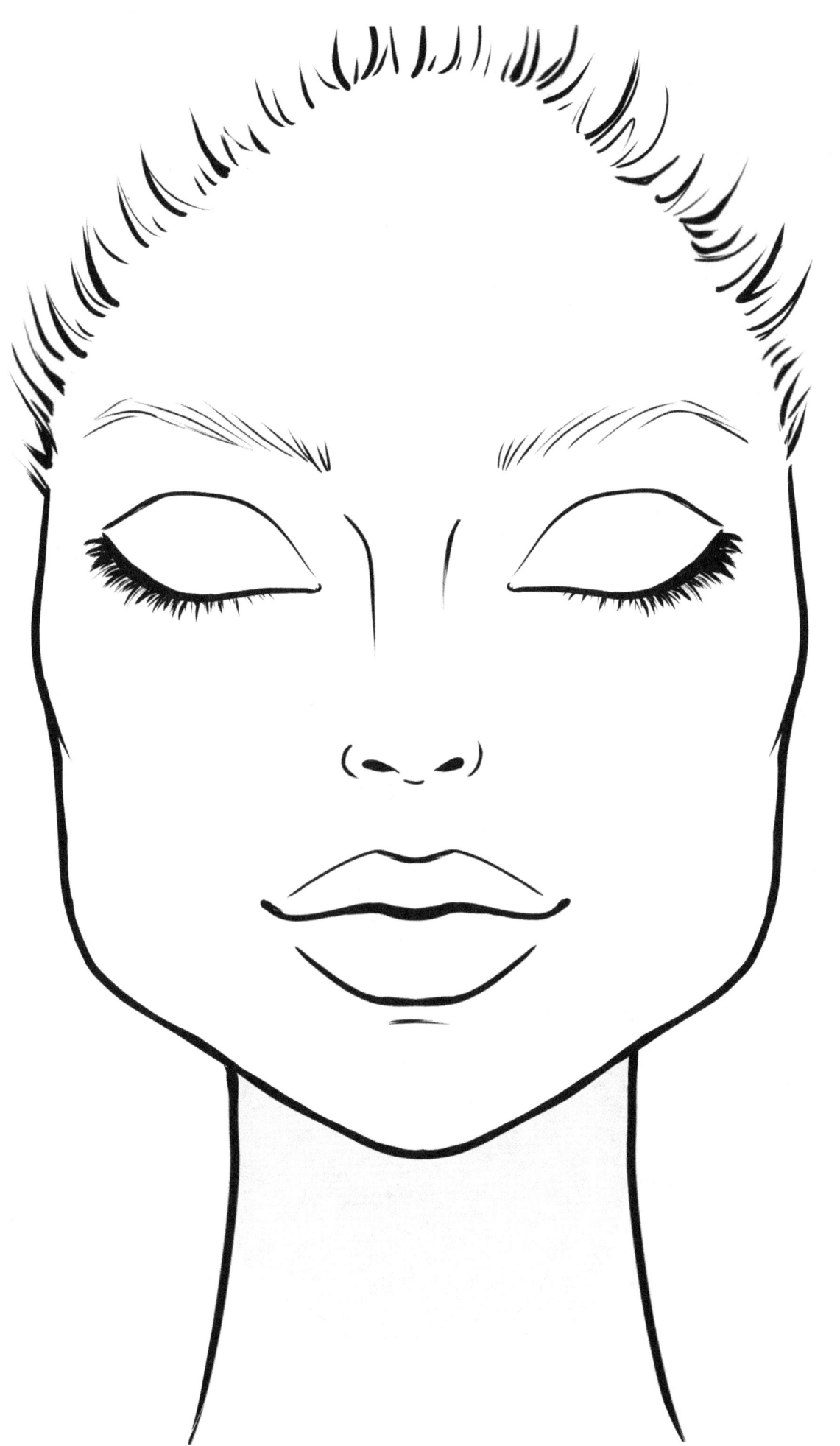

PREPARATION

Cleanser

Moisturizer

Primer

FACE

Concealer

Foundation

Powder

Highlighter

Contour

Bronzer

Blush

EYES

Eyeshadow lid

Eyeshadow crease

Eyeliner

Mascara

Lashes

Brows

LIPS

Lip color

Lip liner

Lip gloss

OTHER

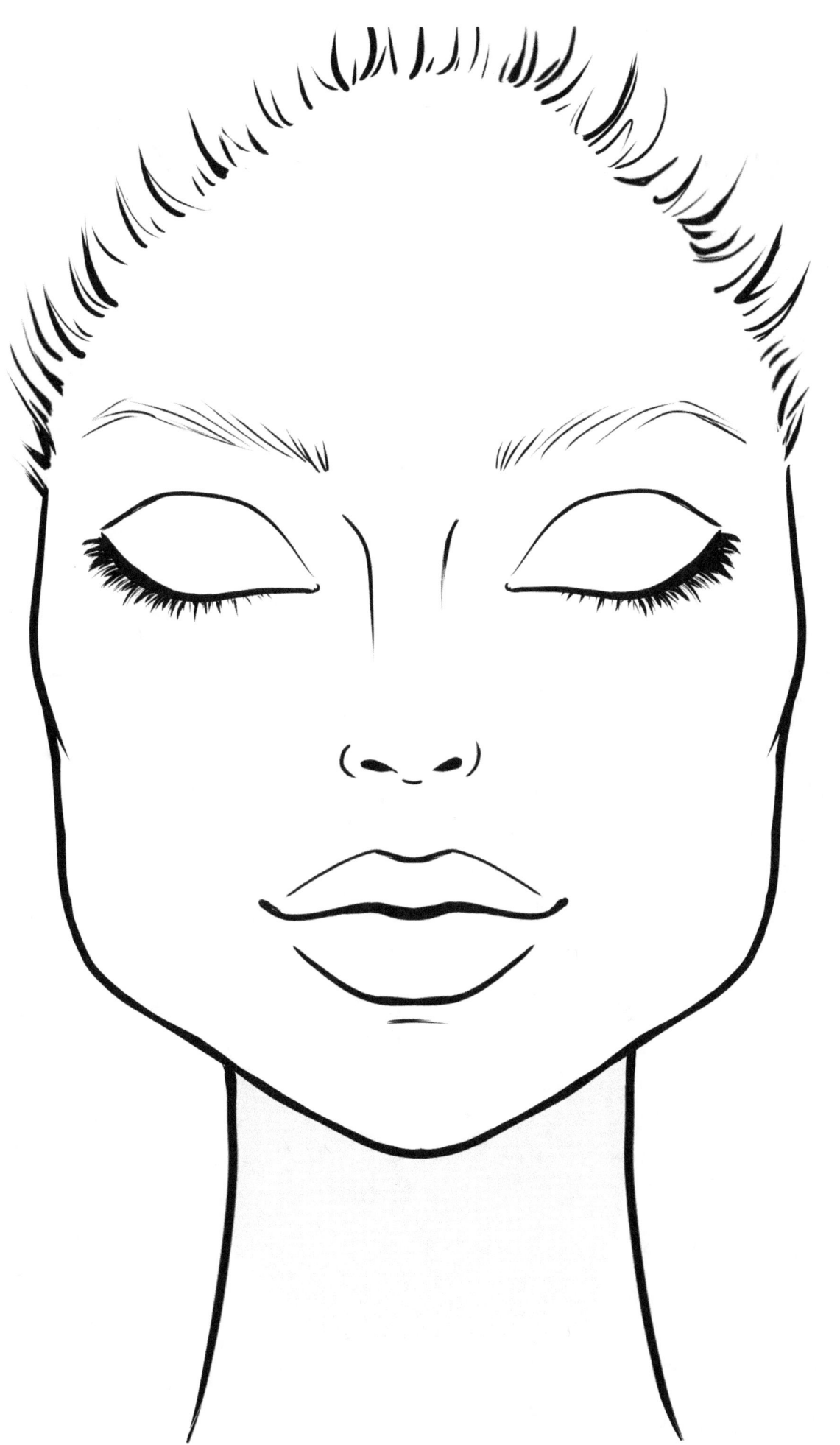

PREPARATION

Cleanser

Moisturizer

Primer

FACE

Concealer

Foundation

Powder

Highlighter

Contour

Bronzer

Blush

EYES

Eyeshadow lid

Eyeshadow crease

Eyeliner

Mascara

Lashes

Brows

LIPS

Lip color

Lip liner

Lip gloss

OTHER

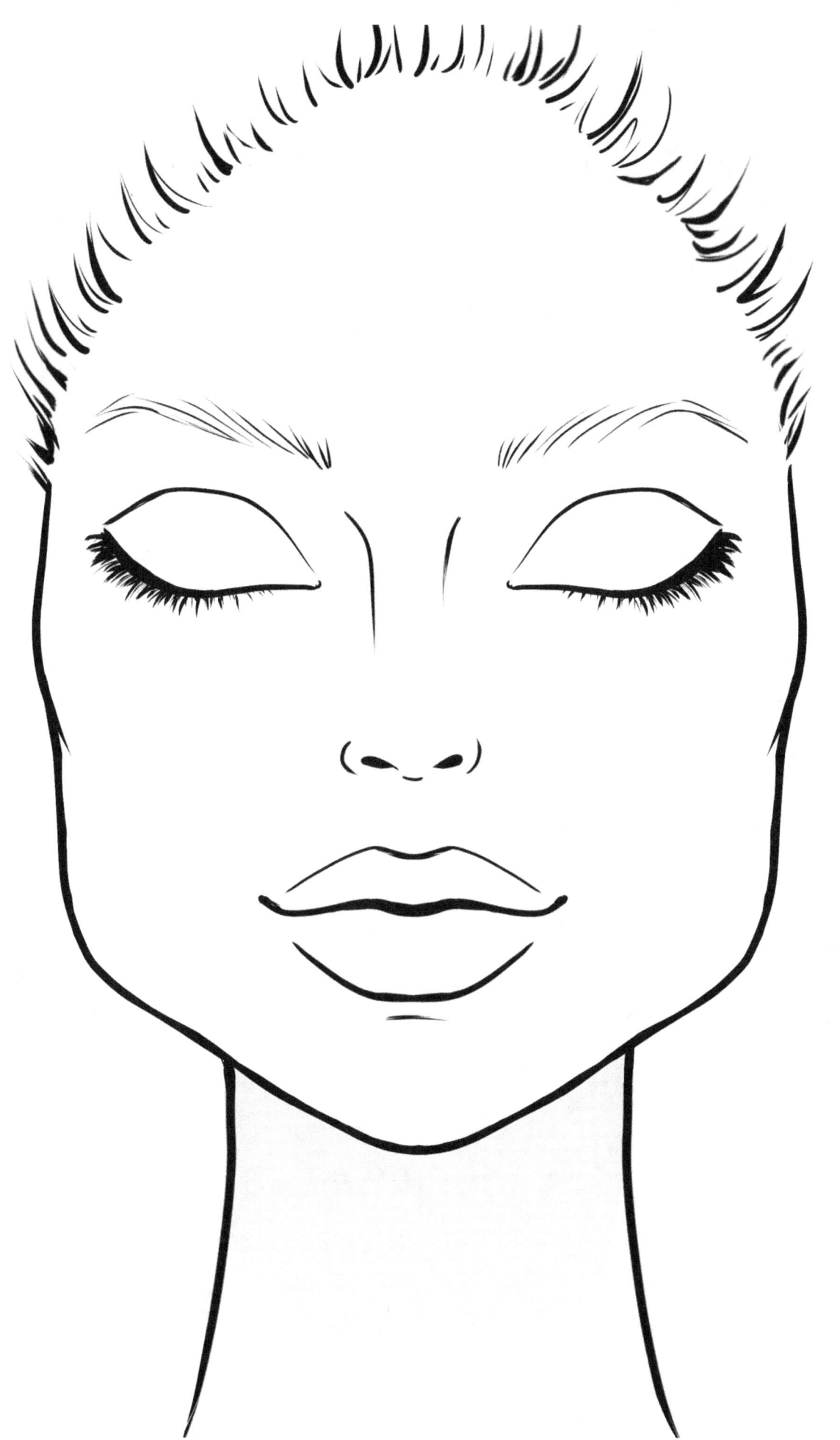

PREPARATION

Cleanser

Moisturizer

Primer

FACE

Concealer

Foundation

Powder

Highlighter

Contour

Bronzer

Blush

EYES

Eyeshadow lid

Eyeshadow crease

Eyeliner

Mascara

Lashes

Brows

LIPS

Lip color

Lip liner

Lip gloss

OTHER

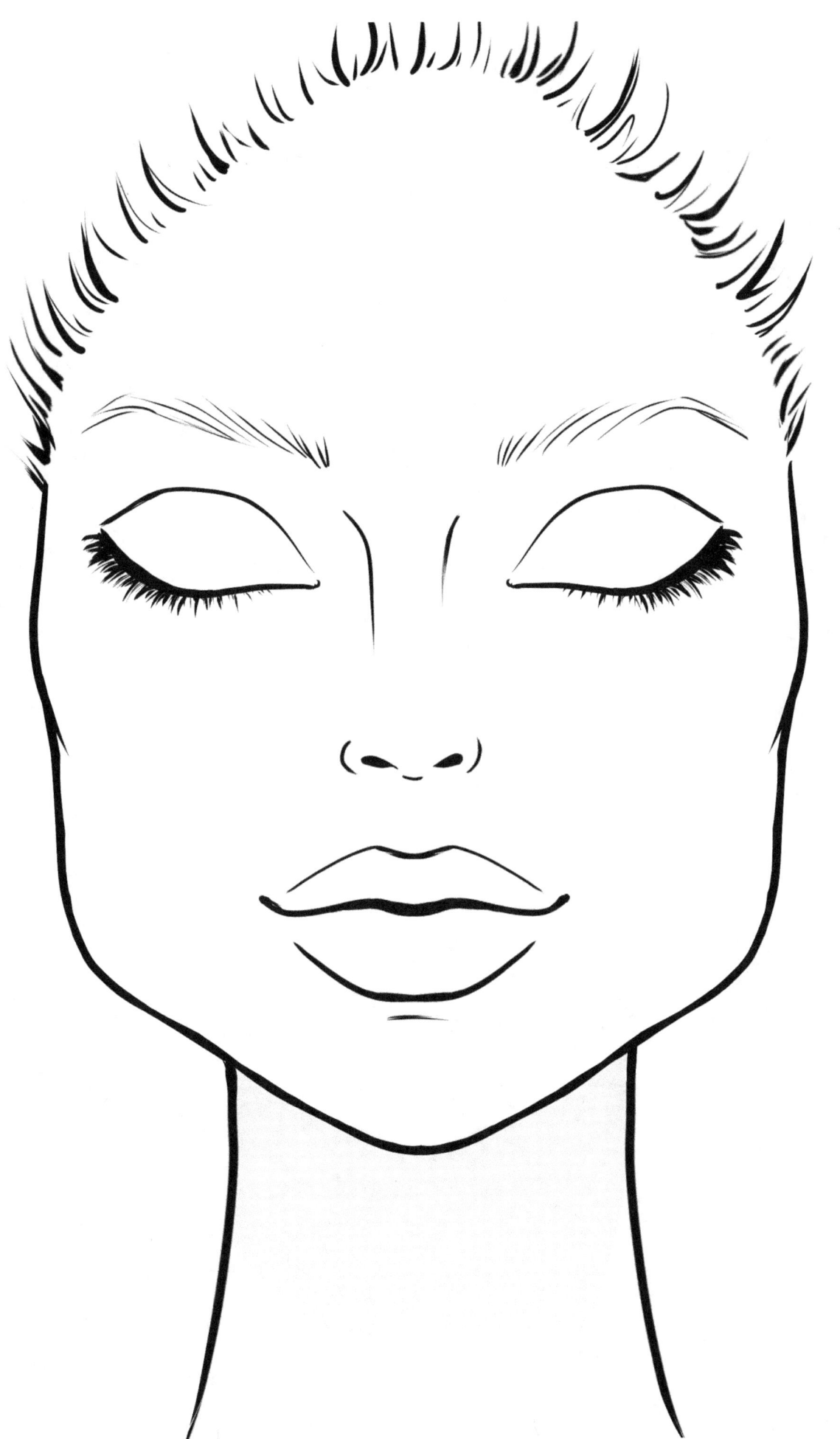

PREPARATION

Cleanser

Moisturizer

Primer

FACE

Concealer

Foundation

Powder

Highlighter

Contour

Bronzer

Blush

EYES

Eyeshadow lid

Eyeshadow crease

Eyeliner

Mascara

Lashes

Brows

LIPS

Lip color

Lip liner

Lip gloss

OTHER

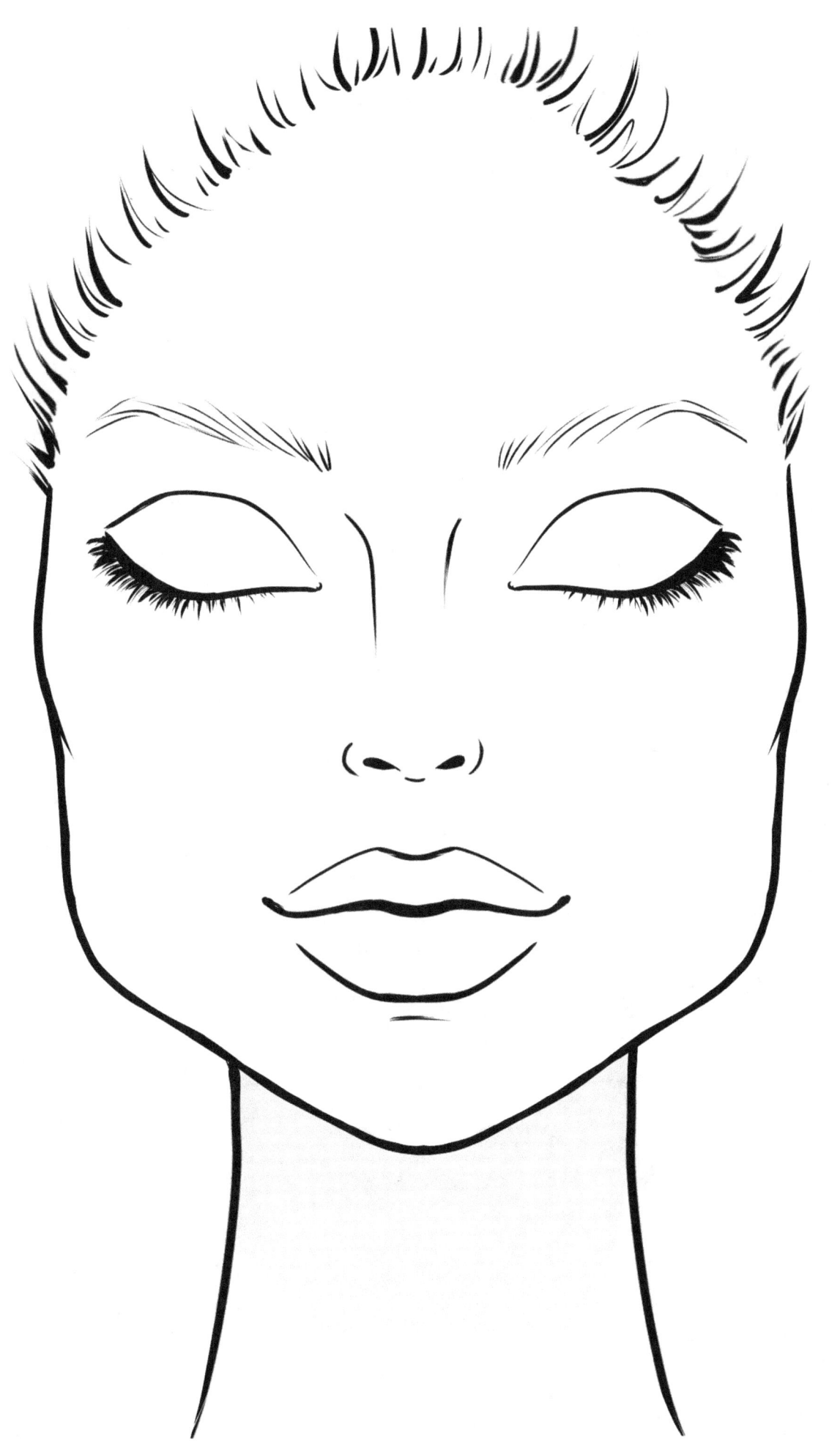

PREPARATION

Cleanser

Moisturizer

Primer

FACE

Concealer

Foundation

Powder

Highlighter

Contour

Bronzer

Blush

EYES

Eyeshadow lid

Eyeshadow crease

Eyeliner

Mascara

Lashes

Brows

LIPS

Lip color

Lip liner

Lip gloss

OTHER

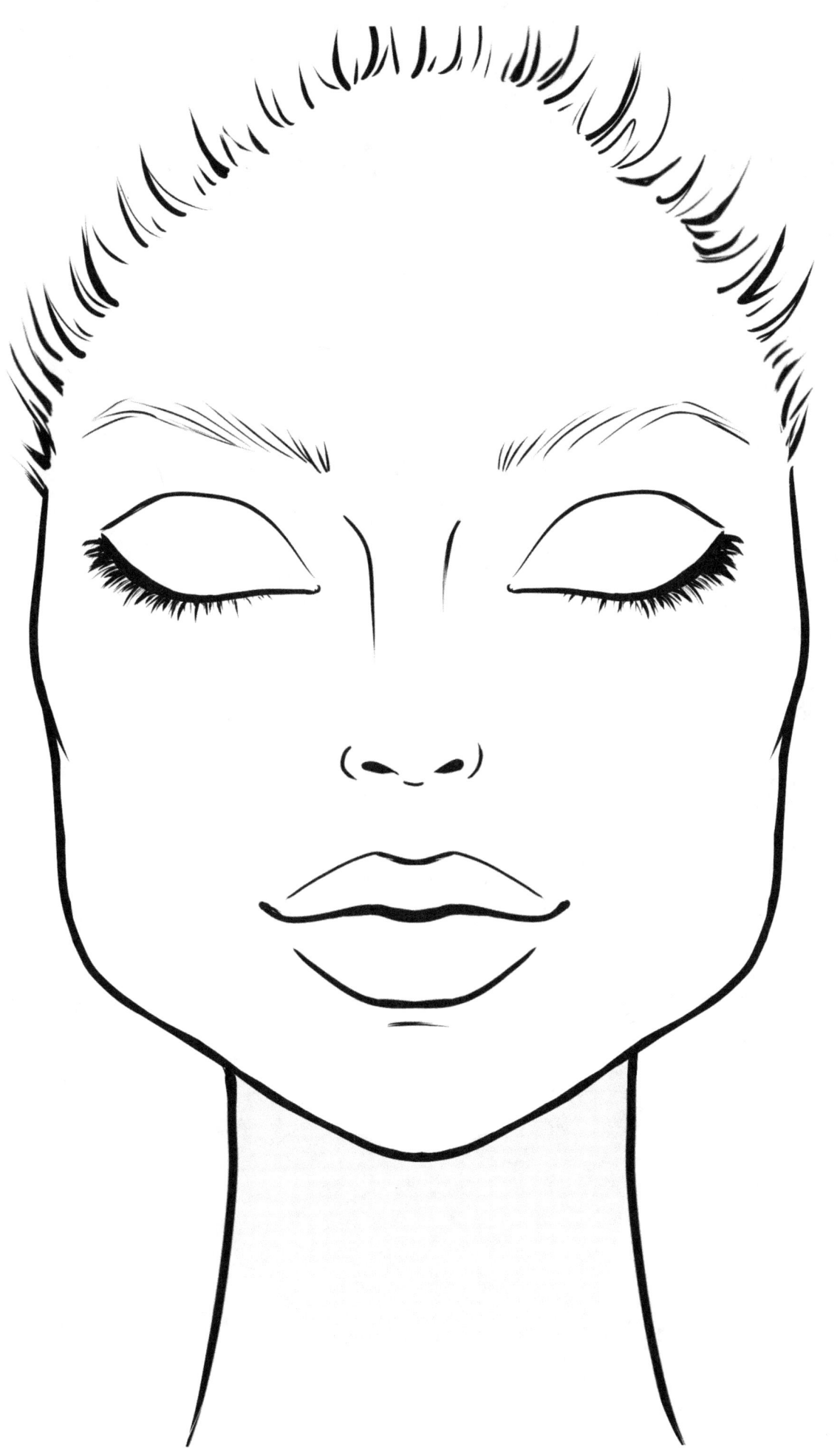

PREPARATION

Cleanser

Moisturizer

Primer

FACE

Concealer

Foundation

Powder

Highlighter

Contour

Bronzer

Blush

EYES

Eyeshadow lid

Eyeshadow crease

Eyeliner

Mascara

Lashes

Brows

LIPS

Lip color

Lip liner

Lip gloss

OTHER

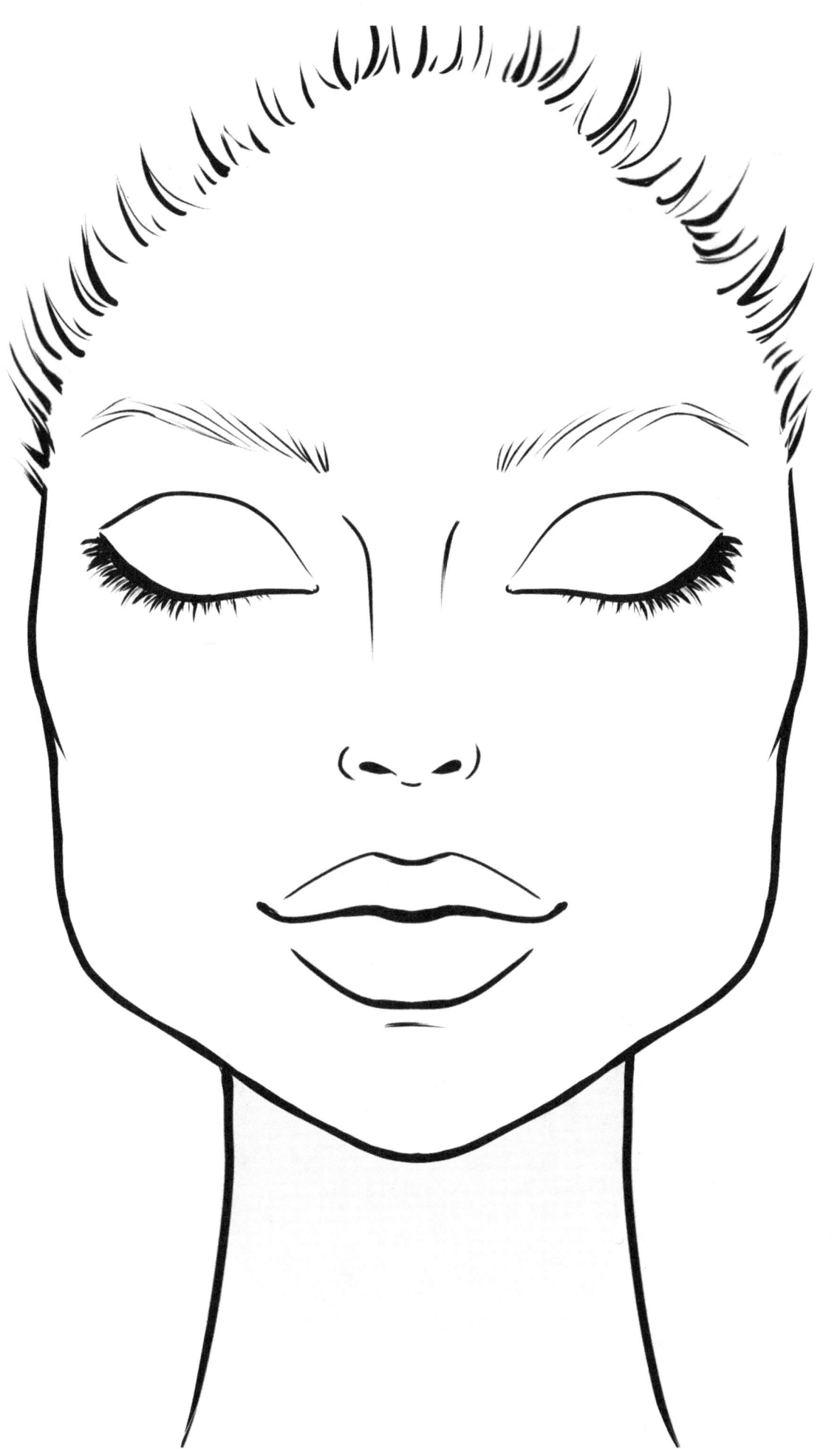

PREPARATION

Cleanser

Moisturizer

Primer

FACE

Concealer

Foundation

Powder

Highlighter

Contour

Bronzer

Blush

EYES

Eyeshadow lid

Eyeshadow crease

Eyeliner

Mascara

Lashes

Brows

LIPS

Lip color

Lip liner

Lip gloss

OTHER

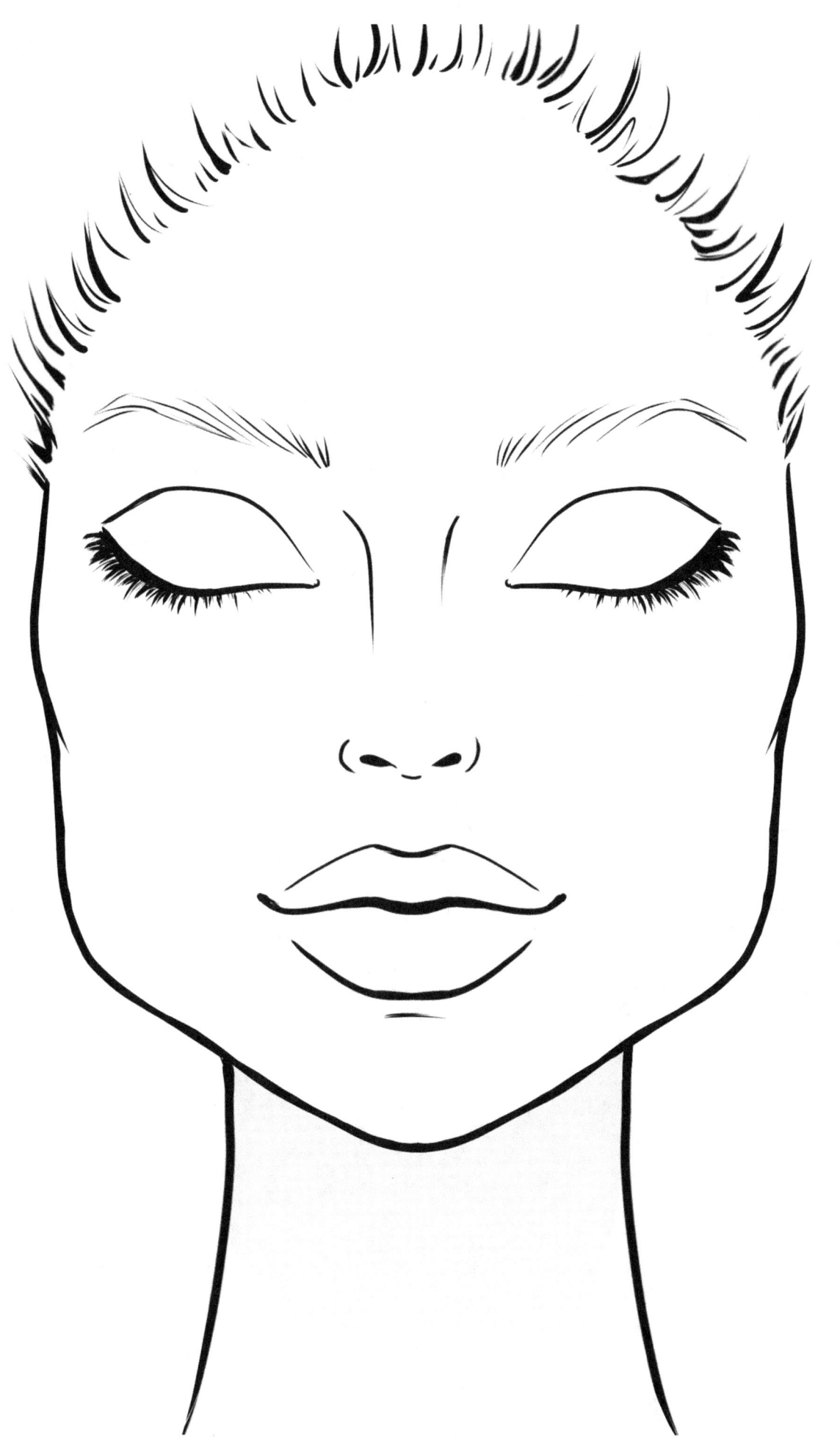

PREPARATION

Cleanser

Moisturizer

Primer

FACE

Concealer

Foundation

Powder

Highlighter

Contour

Bronzer

Blush

EYES

Eyeshadow lid

Eyeshadow crease

Eyeliner

Mascara

Lashes

Brows

LIPS

Lip color

Lip liner

Lip gloss

OTHER

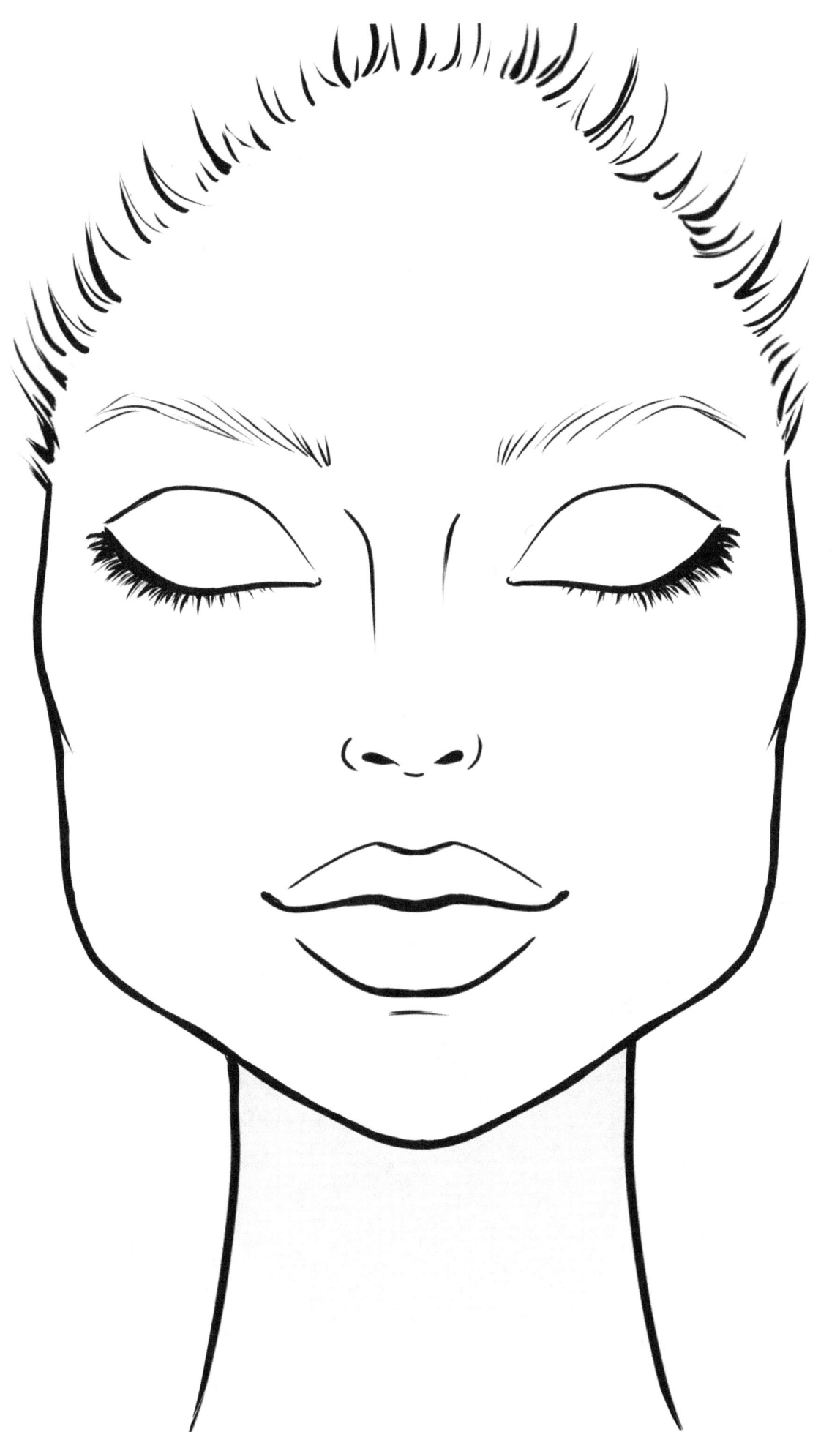

PREPARATION

Cleanser

Moisturizer

Primer

FACE

Concealer

Foundation

Powder

Highlighter

Contour

Bronzer

Blush

EYES

Eyeshadow lid

Eyeshadow crease

Eyeliner

Mascara

Lashes

Brows

LIPS

Lip color

Lip liner

Lip gloss

OTHER

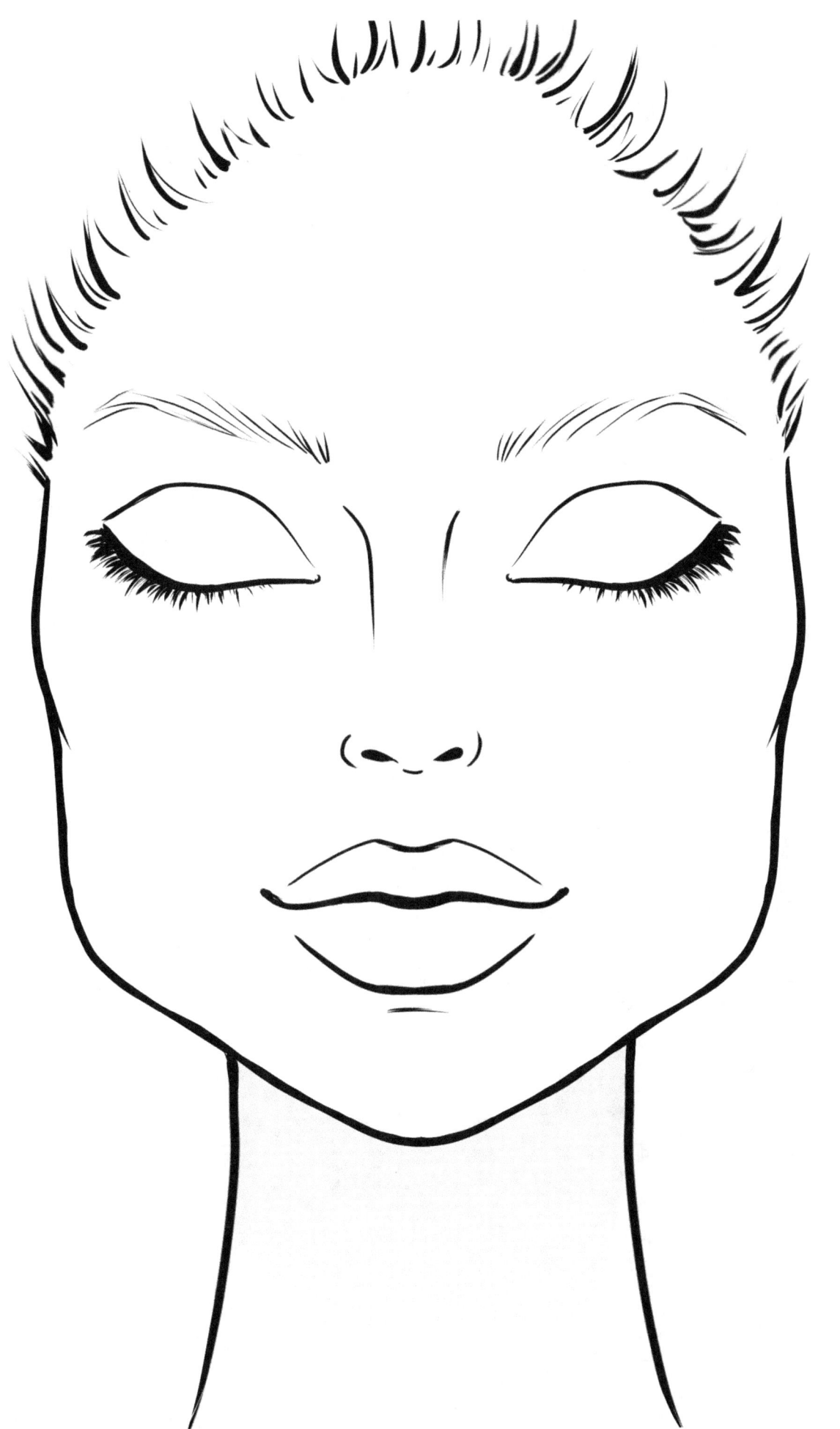

PREPARATION

Cleanser

Moisturizer

Primer

FACE

Concealer

Foundation

Powder

Highlighter

Contour

Bronzer

Blush

EYES

Eyeshadow lid

Eyeshadow crease

Eyeliner

Mascara

Lashes

Brows

LIPS

Lip color

Lip liner

Lip gloss

OTHER

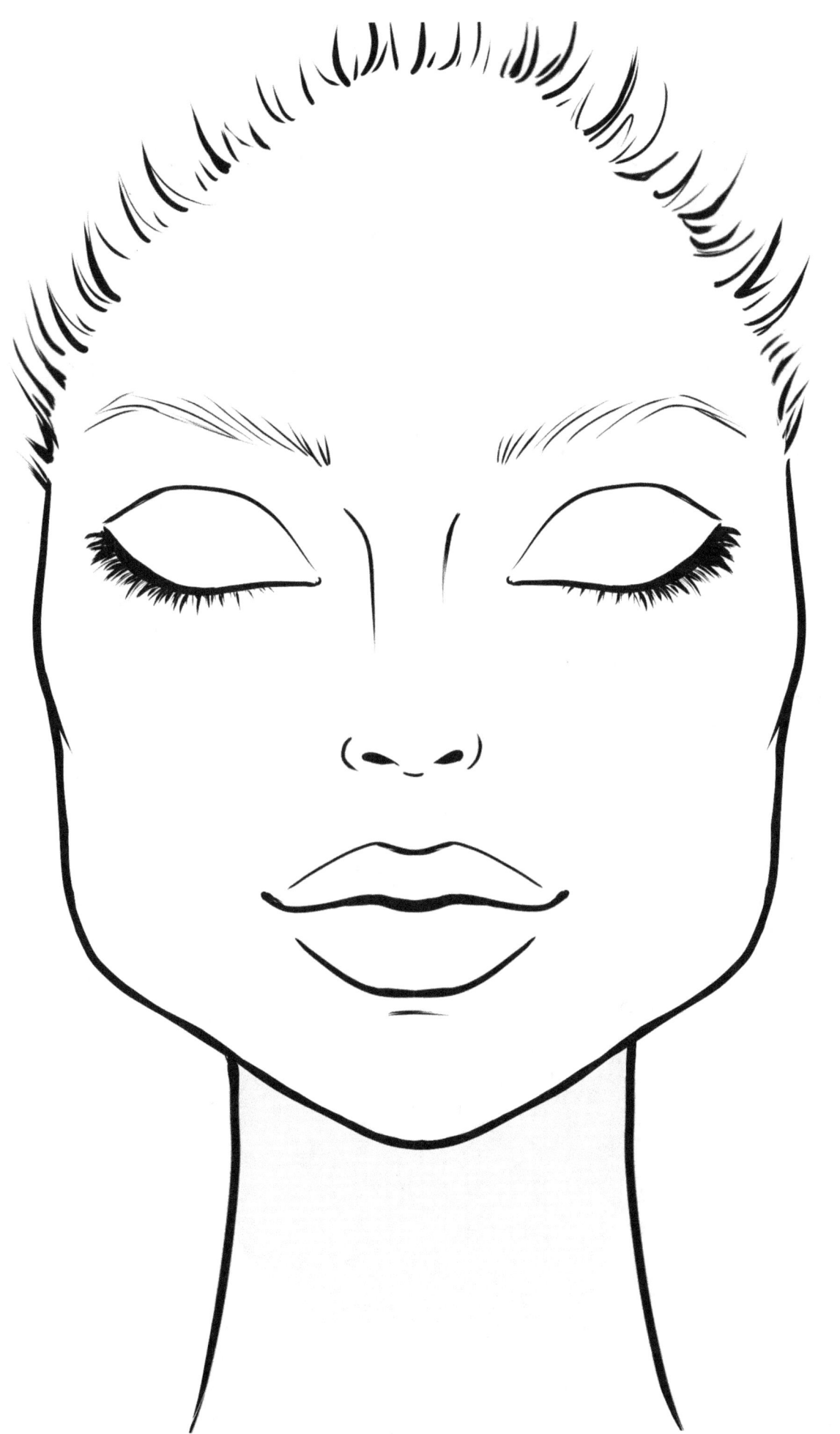

PREPARATION

Cleanser

Moisturizer

Primer

FACE

Concealer

Foundation

Powder

Highlighter

Contour

Bronzer

Blush

EYES

Eyeshadow lid

Eyeshadow crease

Eyeliner

Mascara

Lashes

Brows

LIPS

Lip color

Lip liner

Lip gloss

OTHER

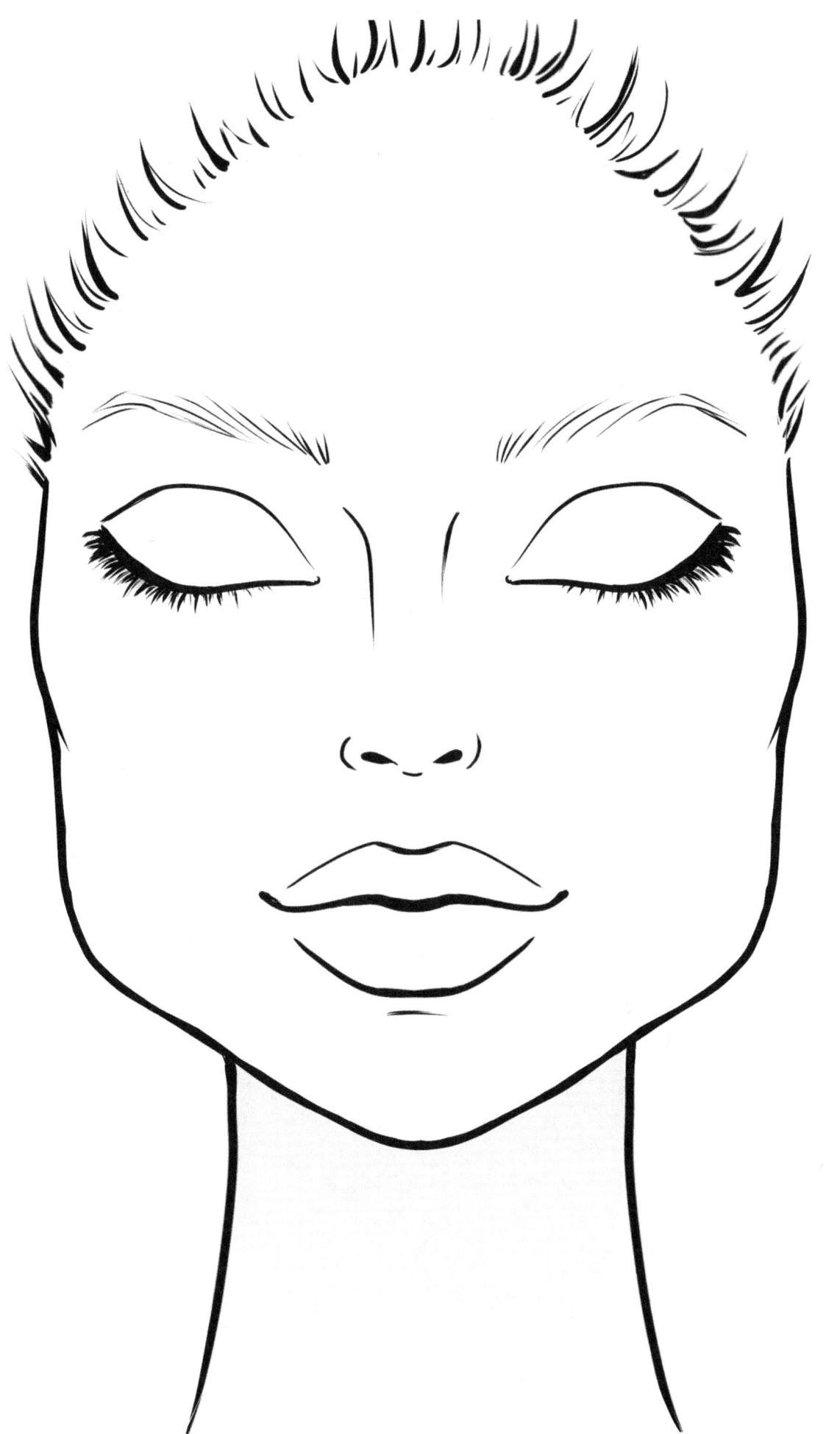

PREPARATION

Cleanser

Moisturizer

Primer

FACE

Concealer

Foundation

Powder

Highlighter

Contour

Bronzer

Blush

EYES

Eyeshadow lid

Eyeshadow crease

Eyeliner

Mascara

Lashes

Brows

LIPS

Lip color

Lip liner

Lip gloss

OTHER

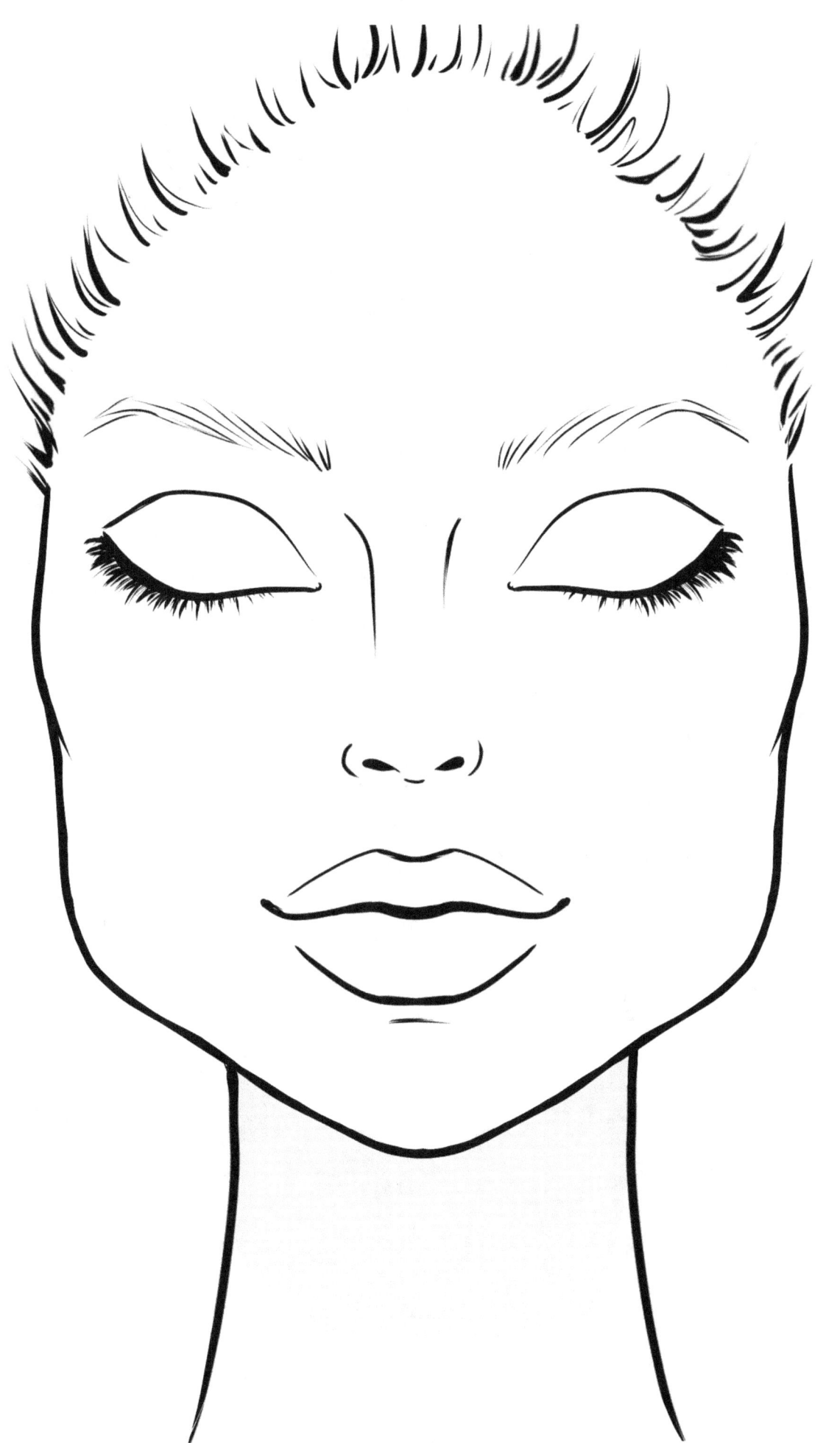

PREPARATION

Cleanser

Moisturizer

Primer

FACE

Concealer

Foundation

Powder

Highlighter

Contour

Bronzer

Blush

EYES

Eyeshadow lid

Eyeshadow crease

Eyeliner

Mascara

Lashes

Brows

LIPS

Lip color

Lip liner

Lip gloss

OTHER

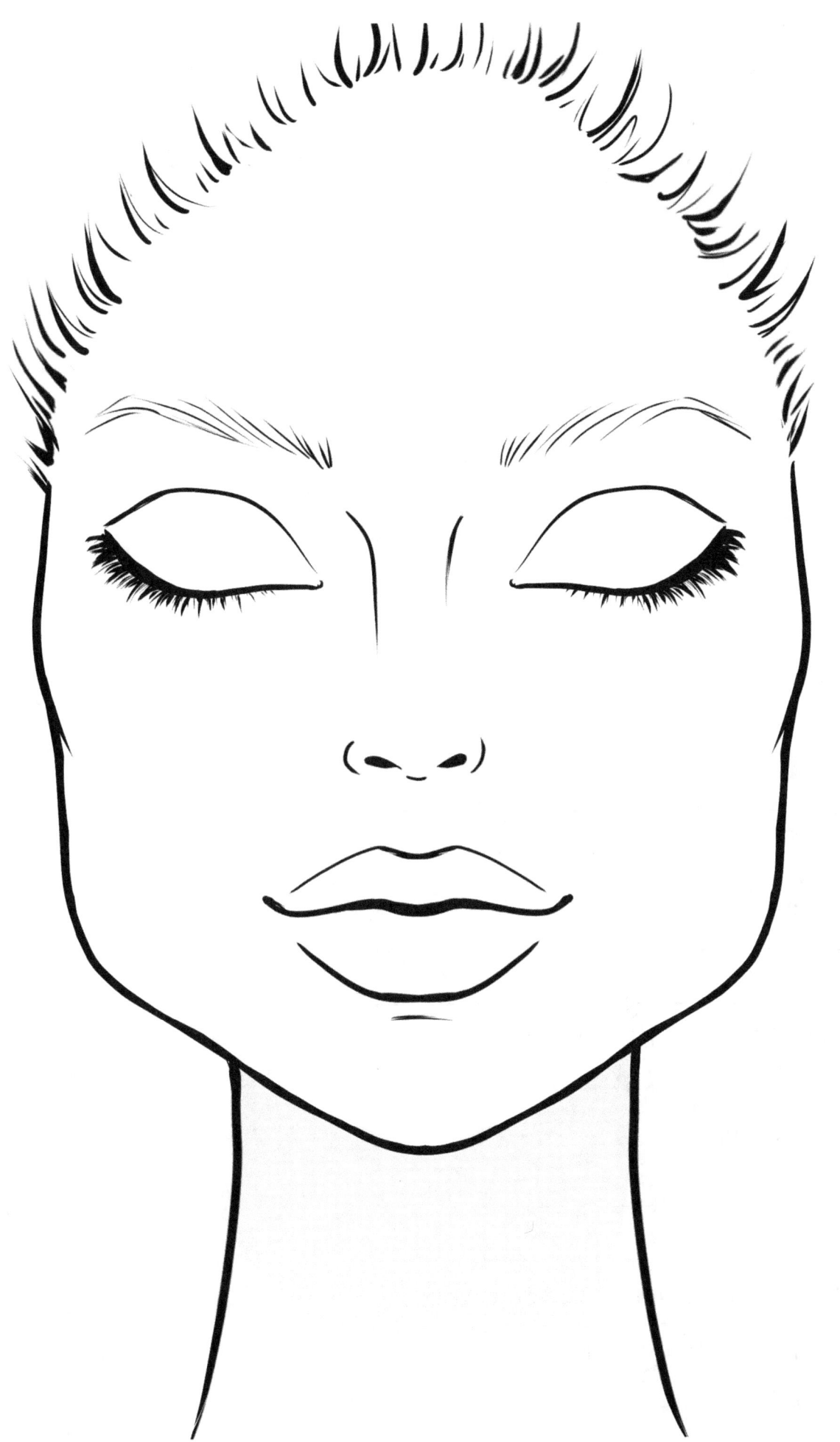

DOWNLOAD FASHION CROQUIS:

WWW.IFASHIONTEMPLATES.COM

FREE STEP-BY-STEP FASHION DRAWING TUTORIALS:

WWW.IDRAWFASHION.COM

FASHION DESIGNING COURSES:

WWW.ACADEMY.IDRAWFASHION.COM

MORE FROM US:

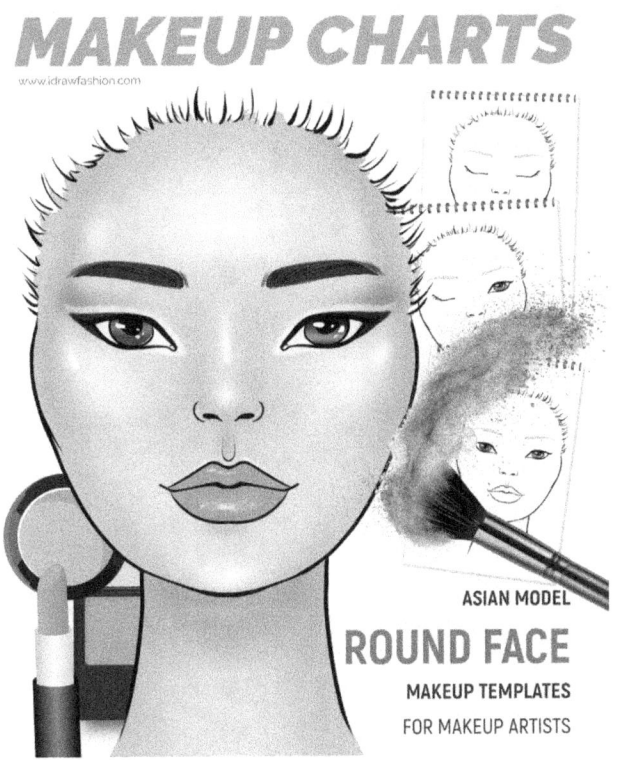
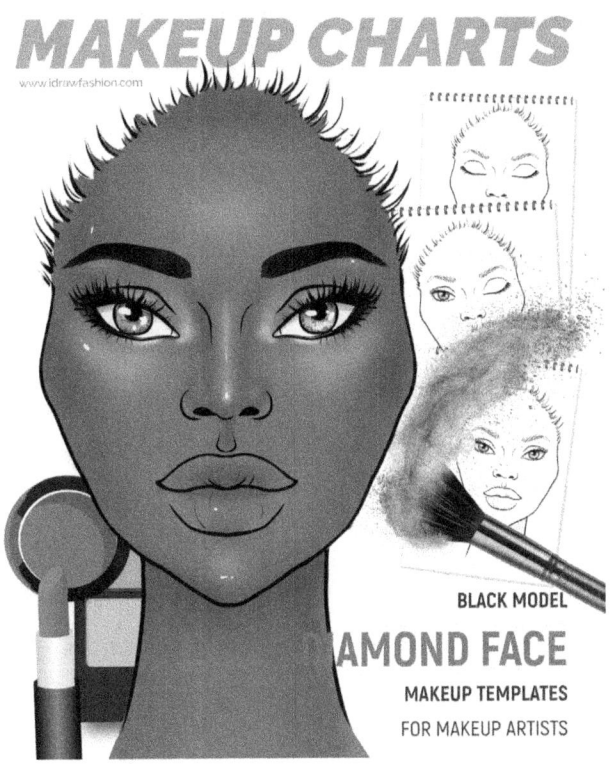
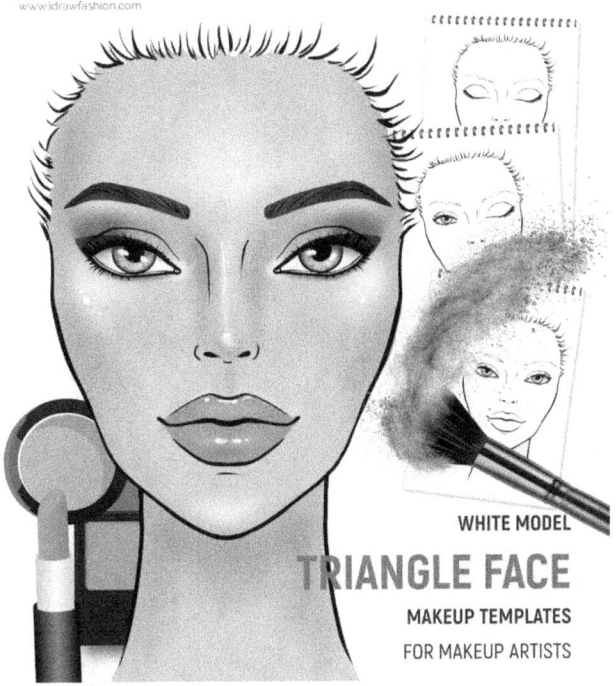
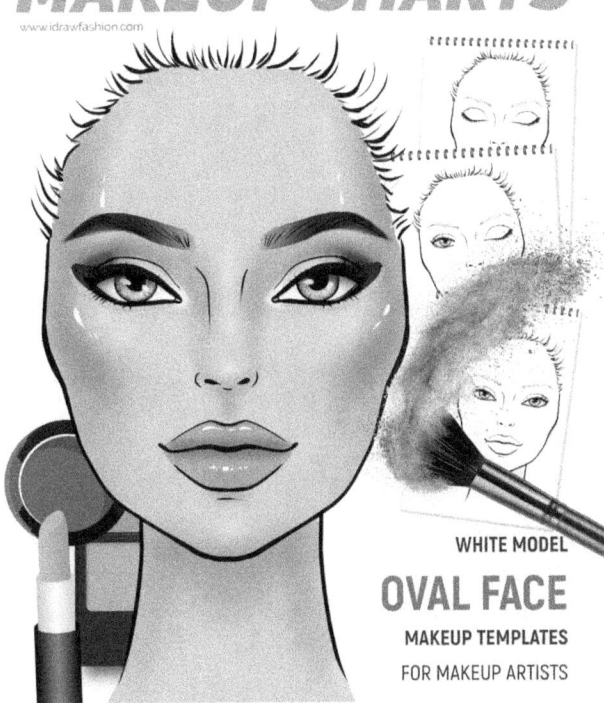

www.ingramcontent.com/pod-product-compliance
Lightning Source LLC
Chambersburg PA
CBHW081434220526
45466CB00008B/2388